Finance

Finance

Other books in the Careers for the Twenty-First Century series:

Aeronautics
Biotechnology
Education
Engineering
Law Enforcement
Medicine
Music
The News Media

Careers
for the
Twenty-First
Century

Finance

By Patrice Cassedy

**LUCENT
BOOKS**®

THOMSON
™
GALE

San Diego • Detroit • New York • San Francisco • Cleveland
New Haven, Conn. • Waterville, Maine • London • Munich

On Cover: Stock traders make deals on the floor of the New York Stock Exchange.

LIBRARY OF CONGRESS CATALOGING-IN-PUBLICATION DATA

Cassedy, Patrice
    Finance / by Patrice Cassedy
      p. cm. — (Careers for the 21st century)
Summary: Examines various positions available in the field of financial services, including the qualifications, training, and opportunities for each.
Includes bibliographical references and index.
    ISBN 1-59018-520-X (hardback : alk. paper)
     1. Finance—Vocational guidance—Juvenile literature. 2. Financial services industry—Vocational guidance—Juvenile literature. [1. Finance—Vocational guidance. 2. Financial services industry—Vocational guidance. 3. Vocational guidance.] I. Title. II. Careers for the twenty-first century.
    HG173.8.C38 2004
    332'.023—dc22

                                                 2003012159

Contents

Foreword

Young people in the twenty-first century are faced with a dizzying array of possibilities for careers as they become adults. However, the advances in technology and a world economy in which events in one nation increasingly affect events in other nations have made the job market extremely competitive. Young people entering the job market today must possess a combination of technological knowledge and an understanding of the cultural and socioeconomic factors that affect the working world. Don Tapscott, internationally known author and consultant on the effects of technology in business, government, and society, supports this idea, saying, "Yes, this country needs more technology graduates, as they fuel the digital economy. But . . . we have an equally strong need for those with a broader [humanities] background who can work in tandem with technical specialists, helping create and manage the [workplace] environment." To succeed in this job market young people today must enter it with a certain amount of specialized knowledge, preparation, and practical experience. In addition, they must possess the drive to update their job skills continually to match rapidly occurring technological, economic, and social changes.

Young people entering the twenty-first-century job market must carefully research and plan the education and training they will need to work in their chosen careers. High school graduates can no longer go straight into a job where they can hope to advance to positions of higher pay, better working conditions, and increased responsibility without first entering a training program, trade school, or college. For example, aircraft mechanics must attend schools that offer Federal Aviation Administration–accredited programs. These programs offer a broad-based curriculum that requires students to demonstrate an understanding of the basic principles of flight, aircraft function, and electronics. Students must also master computer technology used for diagnosing problems and show that they can apply what they learn toward routine maintenance and any number of needed repairs. With further education, an aircraft mechanic can gain increasingly specialized licenses that place him or her in the job market for positions of higher pay and greater responsibility.

In addition to technology skills, young people must understand how to communicate and work effectively with colleagues or clients from diverse backgrounds. James Billington, librarian of Congress, ascertains that "we do not have a global village, but rather a globe on which there are a whole lot of new villages . . . each trying to get its own place in the world, and anybody who's going to deal with this world is going to have to relate better to more of it." For example, flight attendants are increasingly being expected to know one or more foreign languages in order for them to better serve the needs of international passengers. Electrical engineers collaborating with a sister company in Russia on a project must be aware of cultural differences that could affect communication between the project members and, ultimately, the success of the project.

The Lucent Books Careers for the Twenty-First Century series discusses how these ideas come into play in such competitive career fields as aeronautics, biotechnology, computer technology, engineering, education, law enforcement, and medicine. Each title in the series discusses from five to seven different careers available in the respective field. The series provides a comprehensive view of what it's like to work in a particular job and what it takes to succeed in it. Each chapter encompasses a career's most recent trends in education and training, job responsibilities, the work environment and conditions, special challenges, earnings, and opportunities for advancement. Primary and secondary source quotes enliven the text. Sidebars expand on issues related to each career, including topics such as gender issues in the workplace, personal stories that demonstrate exceptional on-the-job experiences, and the latest technology and its potential for use in a particular career. Every volume includes an "Organizations to Contact" list as well as annotated bibliographies. Books in this series provide readers with pertinent information for deciding on a career and as a launching point for further research.

Introduction

Careers in Finance

Finance careers in the twenty-first century are and will continue to be affected by changes in technology and in society. Americans are living longer and expecting more material comforts than ever before and are increasingly at ease with borrowing money to achieve their personal goals and with leaving their debts unpaid when they die. Financial institutions also are continuing to globalize, offering services throughout the world at lightning speed.

These developments include and necessitate the ever-growing importance of technology in the workplace and impact every type of finance job. Companies will seek workers who can implement systems and procedures that work for many different requirements, in many different countries, and that evolve quickly. At the same time machines—ATMs and computers—handle many tasks that bank tellers once performed. Tellers are fast losing positions to customer service representatives (CSRs) who handle personal contact with customers, which, if it occurs at all, is more and more often by telephone or e-mail. Computers are changing the workplace of other finance employees too. Accountants and financial planners are finding new ways to use the Internet to beef up their research about financial markets; stockbrokers can watch stock prices change in real time on computer screens and transmit trades to specialists outfitted with 3-D technology and wireless, handheld computers.

In spite of these changes, selling services—from preparing taxes to making loans to collecting debts—remains the fundamental goal of finance businesses, and employees at all ranks are being called upon to participate in this endeavor. As a way of pushing more and more customers out of credit union and bank lobbies, these institutions are training employees who do work with the public to sell the idea of using banking-from-home options. CSRs and their teller coworkers receive training in online banking and may be expected to try the service themselves, allowing them to better sell Internet banking to customers who visit customer service desks or teller windows. Even debt collectors are getting into the sales act, pitching consolidation loans and other products when they make contact with delinquent debtors.

According to the Bureau of Labor Statistics, the number of workers needed in many finance-related careers should increase by 2010. For collectors who urge people to pay past-due bills, that increase is expected to be 25 percent, pushing the total number of employees in this field to more than half a million. Accountants and auditors comprise a field more than twice the size of collectors, but the growth in those fields is expected to be less—about 19 percent. More and more Americans are expected

Although many financial institutions interact with their customers via the Internet, most banks still employ tellers in order to handle routine branch transactions.

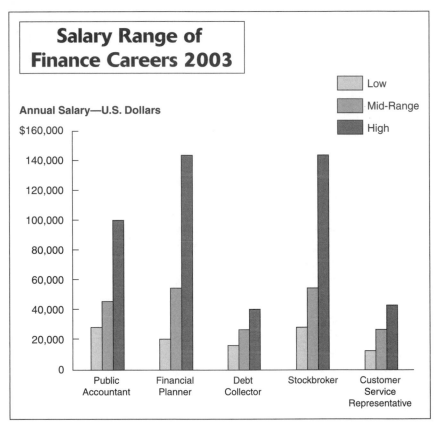

Salary Range of Finance Careers 2003

Annual Salary—U.S. Dollars

Legend: Low, Mid-Range, High

to seek out the services of financial planners, personal advisers who counsel about how to manage money to meet financial goals. Thus this career should increase in size by more than a third to about 125,900 by 2010. Job growth for stockbrokers is expected to be good, with the important caveat that these careers, more than others in finance, are subject to unexpected job loss based on unpredictable changes in the economy or the stock market. Finally those who can assist customers with their banking needs in person or by phone can find jobs as CSRs, a position that should show excellent growth.

Given these trends, banking and finance workers in the twenty-first century will need better technical and interpersonal skills than ever before. In addition, they will have to work harder to keep up with changes in the way financial services are delivered to the public, sharpening their sales, customer service, and technology skills. Those who respond well to change and work hard should find good opportunities in banking and finance.

Chapter 1

Public Accountants

Public accountants work in accounting firms, on their own, or in small partnerships to serve the financial and tax needs of many different individual, corporate, and government clients. The work of public accountants is different from the work of private accountants, who are employees of a single company and take care of financial matters, including budgeting and financial reporting, that relate only to that company. If accountants, whether public or private, are referred to as CPAs, this means they have met rigorous education and testing requirements to earn the designation of certified public accountant in their state.

Public accountants typically work in three different areas: tax, audit, and consulting. They therefore advise on tax issues and complete tax returns, complete independent financial audits (reviews of the accuracy of financial statements, conducted according to accounting and legal standards), and consult on business and accounting practices. Their consulting function is expected to become more important in the twenty-first century due, in part, to a decrease in the need for routine tax work. Technology is at the root of this change because computers allow individuals and businesses to run tax software programs that complete many tasks—such as tracking financial information needed to file paperwork with tax authorities—that were once farmed out to public accountants.

Taxes Matter

In 1789 Benjamin Franklin wrote: "In this world nothing is certain but death and taxes."[1] Indeed taxes—from those that the federal government levies on personal or business income (money

13

made through different sources, including a salary, or profits from selling a product) to a small community's school tax—impact every individual and business in the United States. This is because governmental bodies have the legal power to demand the payment of these taxes. Thus, as expressed by Joel G. Siegel and Jae K. Shim in the *Accounting Handbook*, a tax is a "charge imposed by a governmental body on personal income, corporate income, estates, gifts, or other sources to obtain revenue [money to be spent] for the public good [for example, to build roads, pay military expenses, or provide health care and education]. Tax filing and payment are legally enforceable."[2]

"Legally enforceable" means that if tax payers do not complete and file forms that show the basis for what they owe (or sometimes, that they owe no taxes) and if they do not then pay the taxes that are due, they can have their property taken away to satisfy those taxes, or, in extreme cases, can be prosecuted and jailed. Thus public accountants who help people calculate and pay their taxes are providing an important and serious service.

Benjamin Franklin once quipped, "Nothing is certain but death and taxes."

Most adults understand that taxes are mandatory, but that is where the clarity about taxes ends. How do people and businesses know how much they should pay? Thousands of pages of laws and regulations (plus interpretations made by tax courts and the Internal Revenue Service, or IRS—the agency responsible for collecting federal taxes) describe the complex formulas that determine what is owed. While it would be very simple to set up a system in which a person would pay, for instance, 10 percent of every dollar they earned to the U.S. government, American lawmakers take a different approach. They have structured the tax laws (and constantly change them) to implement policies they deem worthwhile. For example, lawmakers want to make it easier for businesses to succeed. One way of effecting this policy is to help businesses pay for their expenses. Tax laws allow a business to reduce its income (in the eyes of tax collectors) by taking "deductions" from the money the business earns. For example, a musician may be able to deduct the money spent buying CDs because they are used to learn songs that are then played by that musician to entertain people. If the musician made one thousand dollars one year performing at weddings but spent one hundred dollars on CDs, the 10 percent (the "tax rate") would apply to nine hundred dollars instead of one thousand dollars. Thus the musician would owe nine dollars in taxes instead of ten.

Research and Advice

This simple example hardly does justice to the real world of taxes. In fact complexities abound in every detail of taxation. For instance, income tax rates (the percentage mentioned hypothetically above) actually vary a great deal depending on the amount of money earned and whether a taxpayer is a person or company. There is a seemingly endless list of situations in which deductions apply (or might apply, depending on a host of variables), and are calculated. For example if a business buys a certain type of equipment, it may have to spread the deduction that applies to that equipment over a number of years instead of taking the whole expense as a deduction in one year. Helping clients utilize deductions is just one of the many ways that public accountants save taxes for their clients. As explained by Siegel and Shim: "The taxpayer wants to pay the least tax possible. There are many allowable ways of reducing taxes. . . . All tax-saving opportunities have to be used."[3]

The public accountant has a great deal to do to find tax savings opportunities while at the same time making sure clients pay what they should. First and foremost, public accountants must understand what the tax laws provide and be up to date with changes and interpretations of those provisions. To complete this research, accountants spend many hours reading tax codes (collections of tax laws) and interpretations of the laws made by the IRS

A public accountant studies changes in tax laws in order to file a client's tax return.

and tax courts. One of the challenges of this research is that public accountants must be sure that they are looking at the most recent version of the laws and that they are aware of any changes being considered by state or federal tax authorities. As Siegel and Shim caution: "Accounting is a dynamic area that is constantly changing."[4]

Public accountants once waded through notebooks with thousands of loose pages (to allow them to be replaced when they became out of date) to find answers to tax questions. However tax research in the twenty-first century is completed using CD-ROMs and on-line databases that provide legal resources and research tools specifically about taxes and related issues. Public accountants also access websites set up by the federal government. All of these electronic resources can be updated easily and often. In addition, public accountants read professional journals and reference books, in paper form and online, and interact with other professionals in meetings, by phone, or over the Internet. They also rely on websites of professional organizations such as the American Institute of Certified Public Accountants (AICPA).

Meeting Client-Specific Needs

Public accountants conduct general research to maintain their expertise. However the primary function of research is to allow them to give their individual clients specific advice. To be successful at this they must first know what financial factors affect their clients' tax obligations and the nature of their clients' financial

Ethical Behavior

Certified public accountants (CPAs) who join the American Institute of Certified Public Accountants (AICPA) agree to abide by the organization's Code of Professional Conduct. Catherine Allen, senior manager of the AICPA Professional Ethics Division, explains in an interview with the author how these and other rules and laws that regulate behavior help and challenge accountants:

The AICPA's Code of Professional Conduct includes guidelines . . . on such things as integrity, objectivity, competence, due care, and fee arrangements. The rules help CPAs understand that as a professional, they have a responsibility to the public, to clients, and to colleagues. . . . Ethical guidelines are important because they help to define the boundaries of acceptable practice for a professional accountant. [At the same time, ethical] guidelines present many challenges to professionals. First of all, clients do not always wish to follow their CPA's advice, and sometimes what a client wants to do may even be illegal. That forces the CPA to either convince the client to follow his or her advice or to stop performing services for the client. Also, there are many "gray areas" in the rules, meaning there is often no clear right or wrong course of action for a particular situation. These situations require a CPA to apply his or her best professional judgment. The CPA might seek the help of others but the important thing is that he or she considers carefully what the best choice is under the circumstances. . . . "Ethics" [goes] beyond what is required by [the AICPA guidelines or laws that apply to accountants]. . . . There is honor and responsibility in serving the public [as a member of a profession].

goals. This familiarity with clients is at the core of a public accountant's responsibility to competently meet clients' needs. As the AICPA explains, effective tax work requires a public accountant to have "a thorough understanding of the client's business, investment, and personal objectives."[5]

To this end public accountants schedule meetings in their offices or at the homes or offices of their clients. They may conduct interviews by phone or have clients fill out questionnaires that disclose information about earnings and expenses and family changes such as the addition of a child or a family's cross-country move, both of which may trigger tax savings. Of course tax advice given to companies, which have many different sources of income and potential sources of deductions, and many options about how to account for money earned, is far more complex. Public accountants have long meetings with the company's private accountants and with executives and managers in order to review the company's financial situation and its tax-related goals. They also look over financial reports and other documents provided by the company.

Public accountants take all this research and then give advice either verbally or in writing. For a corporate client the advice may take the form of a long memorandum. Advice given to individual clients is typically more streamlined. For example, a public accountant may suggest (in a letter or phone call) that a client buy a house rather than rent an apartment because part of the payments made on the house (the interest on the mortgage) can be taken as an income tax deduction, while rent for an apartment cannot.

Public accountants often suggest ways that clients can better manage personal and business records. For example, to help the musician to document deductions (thus making sure full advantage can be taken of them and that proof of them can be provided to the IRS if necessary), the public accountant may recommend that the musician keep a log of expenses (e.g., the purchase of a new saxophone), the amount spent, and the date of the expenditure.

Public accountants advising companies also look at how taxes are being managed. In *Accounting for Dummies*, John A. Tracy gives this example: "CPAs can advise on which accounting methods minimize taxable income . . . and which business ownership structure can reduce tax bills of the business and its owners."[6]

Filing Taxes

In addition to giving advice, public accountants perform the important function of preparing tax forms that tax authorities (the federal or state government) require individual and corporate taxpayers to file each year. These forms vary from a few pages to many pages and require the public accountant to gather financial information from clients to place into blanks on the forms. This includes written information such as the taxpayer's name and profession but is mostly in dollar form. Thus the public accountant documents how much the taxpayer earned from a salary and other sources, expenses such as purchasing new business equipment or interest paid on mortgages, and money given to charity. Public accountants type these figures into tax preparation software programs that perform mathematical calculations (to total income and expenses and to apply tax rates to taxable income) that were once done by hand or with calculators.

When tax forms are complete, the public accountant sends them to the client for review using fax, e-mail, or regular mail. If the client approves the return, the accountant signs it to show that he or she has prepared it and helps the client file the form by giving instructions about how much should be paid to the tax authorities and by providing an envelope for mailing. In the twenty-first century, public accountants often file tax returns electronically but only after a client has signaled approval in writing. Public accountants maintain files of all information that clients provide and of completed and filed tax returns.

Financial Audits of Companies

A key function of public accountants who have earned the certified public accountant designation is to conduct independent financial audits. An audit is an investigation of a company's business practices and paperwork to show whether or not financial statements released to the public accurately reflect what is going on in the company. This investigation is conducted according to special rules called Generally Accepted Accounting Principles (GAAP). When public accountants finish this investigation, they decide whether or not the company has met GAAP standards and issue a short report stating their findings. These reports are included in larger reports compiled by companies to tell the public about their financial situation. U.S. law requires that companies that sell their shares of stock (part ownership interests in a company) to the public have audits every year.

To complete an audit public accountants take a careful look at the reality behind a company's financial reports. The investigation is very broad and includes a review not only of business records but also of procedures and the day-to-day conduct of business. For example, to audit a candy manufacturer, CPAs travel to the company's main office to look at records that reflect how the business is run. These records include invoices (bills) sent to candy stores that buy candy from the company and purchase orders for raw ingredients (such as sugar or chocolate). CPAs

In order to audit companies like this candy manufacturer, CPAs must visit the company's main office and carefully examine its business records.

examine contracts and agreements, such as those that allow the candy company to rent equipment used to manufacture or package candy. They also visit the company factory to watch how the candy is made and accounted for before it is shipped out. In addition, auditors check whether procedures are in place to minimize theft of company property or secrets (such as a recipe for fudge) by employees or outsiders.

Examining the financial aspects of a business from many angles can take a public accountant on an interesting adventure. One public accountant, Carol Subosits, describes some of the activities she became engaged in while on the "audit trail." Subosits said: "Shortly after I entered the profession, I came to know the very diverse atmosphere which public accounting offered. . . . [I had the chance] to tour coal mines, take midnight inventories at aluminum mills, chase fork lifts at a steel mill, climb silos and chemical tanks, and test-count explosives."[7]

Tasks such as these help auditors tell a story about how well a company is being run and whether its public image reflects what is really going on. Do the purchase orders match a report of what has been bought? Did the amount paid for an item match the bill? Is all of the math correct? Are contracts and agreements reasonable and enforceable? Does the company have safeguards in place to verify that employees follow safety guidelines?

Shari H. Wescott and Robert E. Seiler, accountants and authors of the book *Women in the Accounting Profession*, describe what happens once all the relevant information has been collected and the audit is about to wrap up:

> When this long [auditing] process is concluded, the auditor exercises his or her professional judgment and issues a final opinion about the company in an "audit report." It is hoped that everything checks out O.K., whereupon the report is a "clean" report. If the auditor is not satisfied in all respects, the report will be "qualified," and in extreme cases a "disclaimer" is given to indicate that the auditor cannot express any opinion at all.[8]

Consulting

Consulting is the wave of the future for many public accountants because so many of the more mundane functions they once performed, such as keeping accounting records and preparing tax returns, can now be done by the average taxpayer or by company personnel using computer programs designed for that function. Matt Davis, who works at Microsoft as a marketing manager to the accounting industry, describes the significance of this trend:

> According to a survey conducted by *Accounting Today*, four of the top 10 highest growth accounting firms in the U.S. in 1994 were consulting firms. And that number is growing, as public accountants come to realize that they cannot serve clients by performing rudimentary bookkeeping and tax services. The future of the accounting industry is not in finding the numbers, but in correctly interpreting what the numbers mean, and helping clients define strategies for moving the company forward.[9]

As consultants, public accountants aim to help their corporate clients save money, increase profits, and decrease risks. They use their expertise to uncover inefficient or ineffective business practices and accounting methods and to help companies protect against employee or customer fraud. "Assurance services" is a new service that accountants perform in the consulting arena. According to the AICPA its purpose is to support business decision making by "[improving] the quality of information, or its context, for decision makers."[10] This may involve solving a problem with accounting or information systems that are not meshing as they should, or finding ways to gather information about a company's product and analyzing it to improve that product.

In the twenty-first century, as finance becomes more and more global, public accountants will spend more time consulting with multinational companies. This is a high-pressure practice area that involves giving advice to corporations with potentially billions of dollars at stake. Public accountants who take on this work have a great deal of skill, not only in accounting and tax but also in dealing with business and cultural issues that are unique to international corporations. One major accounting firm, Deloitte Touche Tohmatsu, describes this part of their practice this way: "Our international tax specialists appreciate the

Scrambling for a Role in Business

In the twenty-first century, technology will continue to modify the scope of public accountants' duties. This is because computers and other electronic tools allow clients to handle many basic accounting tasks, such as tracking financial data for taxes, that public accountants once oversaw. In Accountant's Guide to the Internet, *Eric E. Cohen describes how this evolution will challenge public accountants to find new ways to serve clients.*

The proliferation of PCs and easy-to-use personal finance/ accounting software, as well as tax packages, make in-house [financial] reporting easier for small businesses. Business is doing business differently in the 1990s—often electronically. Manual books and records have given way to bar-coded data input. . . . Businesses are using electronic data interchange (EDI) to send quotes, invoices, and payments—not on paper but with bits and bytes. Phone and mail order sales are being conducted instead on the Internet. CPAs have found themselves scrambling to keep up with the advice their clients need.

cultural and business differences on a global basis, and we routinely assist clients in solving complex business issues dealing with cross border transactions [those involving more than one country]."[11]

Beyond the Tedious

As public accounting moves more toward consulting, accountants will experience an improvement in one of the biggest negative aspects of the job—the tedious nature of doing repetitive tasks associated with tax work and audits. Young public accountants in large accounting firms are especially subject to becoming bored because they are assigned the nuts and bolts work. Public accountant Rosalind R. Meyers gives one example: "When a client takes a physical inventory we look at what their people do, we make test counts of what they've done. If the tags on the boxes say they have 1,000 little parts in them, we sample one box and count the thousand parts."[12]

Public accounting often involves tedious work like verifying the accuracy of physical inventory.

Consulting work, by contrast, allows accountants to think creatively in order to find new solutions to their clients' business problems. Public accountants may find a pleasant challenge in using their personal skills to improve a client's profits. Wescott and Seiler explain:

> In consulting there is always a specific problem that the client wants solved, and finding solutions to it permits more creativity, even [for less senior accountants]. Most of the new staff that come into this area have had specialized training, such as in computer science, product engineering, or statistics, and they sometimes have had considerable experience.[13]

Working for Large Firms

Aside from the work itself, public accountants may have positive or negative experiences depending on where they work. Public accountants may work in solo practice, as part of a small- or medium-sized partnership, or at one of the major accounting firms, which may have as many as one hundred thousand employees around the world. Each accounting career path has advantages and disadvantages. Stresses of working in a large firm stem from its structure. As public accountants gain experience and prove themselves to the firm, they are expected to follow a path of promotion to senior accountant, then to manager, and ultimately to partner. If the accountant does not succeed in showing that he or she is worthy of a promotion to the next level, then he or she is most likely out of a job. Making partner is extremely difficult. Jason Alba and Manisha Bathija, in the *Vault Career Guide to Accounting*, caution: "Be sure that you understand the requirements to make partner within any specific firm you join. Also, know that it will likely be much harder than you are told to actually reach such a position."[14]

Public accountants who work in large accounting firms benefit from being associated with a well-known professional services organization and are typically extremely well trained. Nevertheless, coping with the high expectations of their bosses and the competition to prove themselves against other young accountants can result in a young public accountant feeling overwhelmed and unhappy with work. Wescott and Seiler describe the common problem: "The long overtime hours and the stress associated with a constant series of deadlines produce a state of burnout after two or three years in the profession. In fact, there is a frequently used phrase called the 'three-year burnout,' although it is sometimes altered to the 'five-year-burnout.'"[15]

Working for Small Firms

Working for oneself or in a small firm typically leads to less stress from competition with coworkers. Nevertheless, keeping up with new tax laws and other information without the support of the large firm structure can be difficult because accounting laws and practice standards change quickly. In the 1990s an insider at one of the largest accounting firms characterized the fast-changing world of accounting this way: "Knowledge gained in the field today will have practically no value within four years."[16]

Jack Fox, author of the book *Starting and Building Your Own Accounting Business*, recommends forming a partnership with another public accountant by merging two solo practices. He sees several advantages to this arrangement:

> Partnerships can give professionals the chance to broaden their expertise in accounting areas . . . which the sole proprietor may consider . . . a luxury. . . . [For example,] one [partner]

may prefer to handle tax procedures; whereas the other may enjoy serving clients in a consulting capacity. Partnerships also provide the opportunity to expand.[17]

One of the chief differences between working for a large firm and going into practice alone or with a couple of partners is that large firms typically have all the clients they can handle but sole practitioners or small partnerships must find business in order to grow. One way of coping with the challenge of getting new clients is for public accountants to specialize. Areas of focus include, for example, charitable giving (which results in large tax deductions for companies) or in business valuation (the process of finding out what a business is worth). Finding a niche can be a good strategy for a public accountant who prefers small or solo practice. Journalist Cynthia Harrington summarized the advantages this way: "Focusing on one area makes a CPA an expert with national exposure who is called upon to educate other professionals. [In addition, the] subject of the specialty is personally fulfilling."[18]

Networking, by keeping in contact socially with clients or putting on seminars, is another popular route to developing a bigger client base. Fox suggests that becoming active in professional and civic organizations is one of the most effective ways of getting one's name out to potential clients—if one remains highly visible in these groups. "We must participate actively and hold positions of responsibility,"[19] he advises.

While making appearances at meetings helps, public accountants are finding that using the Internet to promote themselves is highly efficient and can make even the smallest firm stand out. Eric E. Cohen, author of *Accountant's Guide to the Internet*, believes that "technology can make the smallest firm look as technologically advanced and sophisticated as the biggest firm. A Web site, an electronic newsletter, and participation in newsgroups can give your firm a strong presence on the Internet."[20]

Education, Experience, and Pay

Public accountants have undergraduate degrees in accounting or in similar fields such as finance or business. They may pursue a master's degree in business administration (MBA) or a tax law degree (Juris Doctorate, or the more advanced Master of Laws

Controllers

While public accountants work in accounting firms, private accountants work as employees of a company. The controller is one of the top private accountants within a company. The controller oversees a company's spending and the payment of its bills, including the payroll (wages to employees), and makes sure that accounting reports and records are completed accurately and on time. The controller works with public accountants who are performing a financial audit of the company to make sure that all necessary information is available. Controllers also implement programs that keep the company safe financially; these include completing internal audits—reviews of business and financial practices to make sure they are in the best interest of the company and comply with accounting standards. In all but the smallest businesses, controllers supervise many other employees who are charged with carrying out the day-to-day tasks to implement the controller's responsibilities. Controllers have the same training as public accountants, may become CPAs, and, if they want to work at the best-known companies, earn masters of business administration (MBA) degrees. Controllers can earn well over one hundred thousand dollars a year if they work for very large companies, but small companies pay in the range of fifty thousand dollars.

degree), which some employers prefer or require. Public accountants may become licensed CPAs. CPAs are highly respected because they have completed an extremely rigorous course of study to become certified. In addition to completing coursework—which, in most states, includes thirty hours of study beyond the usual undergraduate program—CPA candidates must pass a four-part uniform CPA examination and have a prescribed amount of public accounting experience. The CPA exam is extremely difficult, and many attempt only parts of the exam at a given time. According to the *Occupational Outlook Handbook*, only one-quarter of those taking the exam pass all the parts they take.

Those in the profession suggest that students gain experience by working as interns in companies or accounting firms. These programs typically offer either modest pay or course credit. Some employers put significant effort into creating programs that provide positive experiences for interns. For example, a firm may offer the intern exposure to a variety of tasks and close supervision by a seasoned mentor. A student can benefit from these programs in more than one way. In addition to getting an inside look at the profession, interns can "show off" to a prospective employer. Because making a good impression will garner at least a good reference and, at times, a job offer, interns are advised to exhibit professionalism and enthusiasm on the job. Andrew Denka, who runs a service that provides temporary staff accountants, gives this specific advice to those working as interns: "Take the initiative to help others on your team [and] . . . abide by all company policies and procedures."[21]

While career paths for accountants vary, almost all accountants have the opportunity to make good money. According to the U.S. Bureau of Labor Statistics, in 2001 the median annual income for accountants was $45,400 with the lowest paid making about $29,000 and the highest paid making about $80,000 or

Public accountants have undergraduate degrees in accounting or in similar fields. Many continue their education and pursue advanced degrees.

higher. Partners in accounting firms make $100,000 and up. A survey by the National Association of Colleges and Employers showed that in 2001 beginning accountants with master's degrees made nearly 10 percent more than those with only bachelor's degrees.

Enthusiasm a Must

Public accountants of the twenty-first century still need the qualities public accountants have always needed, including patience, excellent mathematical skills, and a keen attention to detail. As the profession changes to keep up with technology and globalization, one classic character trait remains more important than ever. CPA James A. Cashin phrases that quality this way: "The one quality which is a prerequisite for a successful accounting career is enthusiasm. You must have an eager attitude and a genuine desire to do the best job you can."[22]

Chapter 2

Financial Planners

Financial planning is a relatively new career that was launched in earnest in the 1970s. The field is described by the Certified Financial Planner Board of Standards, Inc. (which sets standards for certification of financial planners) as "the process of meeting your life goals through the proper management of your finances."[23] To that end planners, who may or may not be certified, meet with clients and find out about their financial situation and personal needs. They help clients define financially related goals for the future—for example paying for their children's college education or enjoying a comfortable retirement. They then develop and help implement plans by working with other finance professionals, including insurance salespeople and stockbrokers. Some planners have licenses that allow them to sell these products themselves. Financial planners may also help with business matters for small or large companies. Planners may work in-house for financial institutions that provide consulting services to customers, in financial planning firms, or on their own.

Sizing Up a Client's Needs

Financial planners help people by acting as sounding boards for financial decisions and by developing plans that help people meet their financial goals. Financial planners are like orchestra conductors: They keep the different "instruments" of their clients' financial lives in tune with each other. Thus they help with budgeting (cash-flow management) and investing (using money to make more money). They give advice on how much to save for their children's college education, for retirement, and how much life insurance to purchase. Financial planners believe that each of these areas of a healthy financial life is best handled in tandem with the other areas. For example, helping clients understand how much money they need to save to pay for the type of college education they want for their children leads to a helpful understanding of how much the clients can afford, after their monthly deposit into college savings, for a house, cars, food, and entertainment.

At the same time, financial planners consider any factors that might interfere with clients' financial well-being. This "risk management" includes counseling on how much life insurance the family wage earners should have in case one of them should die and his or her income needs to be replaced. Journalist Shelley A. Lee interviewed one of the first financial planners and summarized his description of the practice he started in 1974: "Financial planning, says [John T.] Blankinship, was a [new] way to bring the many divergent aspects of a client's financial life together into a coordinated, integrated whole."[24]

Telephone conferences help financial planners identify their clients' needs.

Because planners direct their services to highly specific needs of their clients, they must, in the first instance, discover what those needs are. To that end they interact with their clients on the phone, by e-mail, and through letters, but they almost always begin with an in-person conference that is an hour or two long and typically occurs in the planner's office or conference room. Some planners set the stage for their first meeting with clients by getting basic information beforehand—by sending the client a questionnaire or asking questions over the telephone. Planners use this information to try to get a sense of the client's financial personality, including how much financial risk the planner should build into the client's plan. For example, some clients are willing to invest their money to buy shares of stock—an ownership interest in a company—because even though they risk losing their original investment if the company does not succeed, they can make big returns (the amount they earn above what they initially put in) on their money if the company does well. Other clients prefer conservative investments such as certificates of deposit at banks, because even though the percentage of interest that they earn on the money is relatively small, their original investment cannot be lost. However, even well-crafted surveys may not capture the client's true attitudes. As financial planner Dixie Butler explains: "Clients will say one thing in a questionnaire, then when you discuss investments with them, you sometimes get a different picture."[25] For this reason experienced planners use a client's written responses to stimulate discussion rather than to form conclusions.

During the meeting the financial planner sizes up the client and listens carefully to what he or she (or they, since couples often visit planners together) says about their personal situation and goals. Planners attempt to identify what is wishful thinking, such as an unrealistic expectation about how much money a client can afford to borrow to buy a house. In this way financial planners help clients stay on target for bigger goals, such as having enough money left over at the end of the month to save for retirement. The planner elicits answers to many questions about clients' assets (money they have and property they own), debts (money they owe), and income (money they earn at work or on investments).

Planners also ask questions that help define what the client expects from the financial planning relationship. What does the client need to know at this time? What information might be useful in the future? With this information in hand, the financial planner can begin drafting a financial plan for the client.

Devising a Plan

The Certified Financial Planner Board of Standards, Inc. gives this overview of the purpose of the financial plan and the importance of personalizing it for each client:

> The financial planner should offer financial planning recommendations that address your goals, based on the information you provide. The planner should go over the recommendations with you to help you understand them so that you can make informed decisions. The planner should also listen to your concerns and revise the recommendations as appropriate.[26]

To carry out this responsibility, financial planners put together a long letter or a notebook that is referred to as a financial plan. This document reviews the client's financial and plan-related personal information and contains recommendations the financial planner makes based on that information. Charles E. Foster II, a certified financial planner with years of experience, reports that his plans typically begin with two important sections: a statement of the client's goals and objectives (becoming financially independent by age sixty, for example) and a summary of action items that are gleaned from the more detailed sections of the report. Foster gives these examples of action items a report may contain: "Sometimes clients have too much life insurance and we recommend that they reduce the amount of life insurance. [In another case] we may recommend that the client put more money into a work retirement plan."[27]

Foster's plan has several detailed sections that follow the summary, including, for instance, reviews of the client's current financial status—how their money is invested and what the client owns and owes. Sections on life insurance focus on whether a client has enough (or too much) coverage, whether the type of life insurance is the best given the client's age and family needs, and whether the client is paying a fair price for the insurance they do have. Foster also reviews estate planning documents such as wills and trusts, and points out any concerns the clients might want to raise with their attorney.

While the plan is an important document, it is far more valuable if it is revised on a regular basis to meet the client's changing needs and financial situation. "Keeping the plan up to date becomes more important than [creating] the original plan,"[28] Foster says. This is because the plan is finalized usually weeks or months after the original interviews with the client. Because so many things can change in the financial world in such a short time—the stock market or the client's income can go up or down, for example—a plan can be obsolete almost as soon as the financial planner delivers it.

One planner, Diane Armstrong, developed a system that allows the plan to be conveniently updated at future meetings. She compiles in a binder the plan, notes from earlier discussions, and other documents prepared for the client. Armstrong explains: "We have clients bring [the binder] to the meeting to update it, swap out the old pages and put in new ones. It's a way to help them keep on track toward reaching their goals."[29]

The original plan and revised versions contain recommendations for action that, if agreed to by clients, are implemented by

A planner discusses a financial plan with his clients. Planners must devise flexible financial plans to meet their clients' changing needs.

financial planners or, with the guidance of planners, by other professionals. For example, suggestions about revising a will are referred to an attorney, and specific tax planning issues are referred to public accountants. Financial planners may become licensed to sell some of the products they recommend, such as insurance or stocks. In that case the planner will execute those action items and receive a commission. However, many financial planners are fee-only planners, meaning that they charge an hourly rate for their services rather than commissions on financial products clients buy. In these cases, most typically for the purchase of insurance or stocks, clients will—at the recommendation of the financial planner—turn to licensed insurance salespeople and stockbrokers to implement those portions of the plan.

Once the relationship is established, the planner and client decide how often follow-up meetings will take place and where. Some planners go to the offices of clients. One even flies to Florida once a year to see clients who spend the winter months in the warmer climate. Most planners have opinions about how frequently follow-up meetings should occur. Some opt for a single annual meeting, while others prefer as many as four. Some planners take the lead from their clients. Kelly Christiansen says: "We stay in periodic contact with clients and let them drive the decision as to when they need a meeting."[30]

Making It Personal

Creating plans requires that financial planners synthesize a variety of financial information. Thus planners must be analytically and mathematically minded. However, being able to relate to and communicate with clients is, according to many of the best planners, the most important quality. This is because exploring a client's financial and family situation to arrive at what is financially best can become highly personal. As Foster describes his experience with clients: "They share their hopes, dreams, and worries, [including things] they do not even tell their minister, priest or rabbi."[31]

Because the professional relationship can become so personal, financial planners must work hard at making personal connections with their clients. They do this by being good listeners and by showing their personal interest in the client by, for instance, keeping track of family milestones such as weddings or graduations

A Rosy Future

In the twenty-first century, financial decision making will become more and more complex. This is due not only to the variety and number of financial products available, but also because Americans are living longer and will, therefore, need more savings to support them during their retirement years. In 1998 the results of a study sponsored by the International Association for Financial Planning, now called the Financial Planning Association, showed that younger Americans were more likely to seek the advice of financial planners, while older Americans seeking financially related counseling preferred the services of stockbrokers—professionals who sell stocks and other investments and recommend purchases to their clients. The financial research firm that completed the study suggested that the results bode well for financial planners because as young investors get older and accumulate more wealth, they are likely to continue to prefer to receive advice from, and buy financial products through, financial planners.

and chatting about them with clients when they come in. For Michael B. Horwitz the key to bonding with clients is to let them know that he is a real person too. He does this by sharing a bit about himself, as he explains:

> Sure, my clients think I am "smart," have the proper credentials, and can use the professional jargon. But my clients also know that I grew up in Washington, my dad was a refrigerator mechanic, and my wife teaches at the local university. They know I like to talk about world politics, go hiking in Big Bend National Park, and discuss the meaning of life. I also use my sense of humor and like to laugh a lot.[32]

Marketing Their Services

Good interpersonal skills are also important because planners must be effective at marketing their services in order to develop a client base. Financial planners use a number of techniques to do this. One way is that they mail invitations to prospective customers for seminars on a specific subject—on how to save and invest money for retirement, for example. While some financial planners buy mailing lists that are compiled by companies according to demographics such as age, income, or residence, experts in marketing do not always endorse a broad-brush approach to getting the word out. Martin R. Baird, a marketing expert who wrote *The 7 Deadly Sins of Advisor Marketing*, suggests that financial planners take the time to identify the types of people who might be interested in their services, then tailor a get-acquainted event to them:

> The better you have defined your market, the easier it will be to market to this audience. When you know your target market, you can see them, touch them, hold and feel them. And you won't make the mistake of conducting, for instance, a seminar in an upscale restaurant, when in fact a more low-key, family-oriented restaurant would be more suitable to their temperament.[33]

Financial planners tailor their marketing strategies to specific groups, called target markets. These groups include doctors, dentists, or retirees like this man.

Examples of target markets include retirees or those in a specific profession such as dentists or doctors. Doing a good job for one member of a professional association may mean lots of referrals to other members. This is especially helpful because even though financial planners thrive on referrals, they do not always feel comfortable directly asking their clients to mention their skills to others. Certified financial planner Donald Rembert Sr. expresses a common ambivalent attitude this way: "We're reluctant to ask our clients for [referrals]. We are constantly wrestling with this. We take the position that we offer the highest caliber of advisory services that exists, and that our client base is all the advertising we need."[34]

Financial planners may hire professional marketing consultants not only for advice on defining a target market but also to help them develop a letter or marketing packet that will be most effective. In "Marketing Tactics Examined," journalist Jacqueline M. Quinn summarized the suggestions of Baird:

> Don't underestimate the importance of personalizing your direct mail campaign. . . . For one, sign any computer-generated letter with blue ink. Moreover, be sure to include a personal note on the letter and hand-address the envelope. . . . Use postage stamps. They are preferable over bulk mail, even if the latter is less expensive. Postage stamps remind the reader of mail received by family and friends.[35]

A Second Career for Some

Because financial planning is a relatively new career, many who work at it today did not take courses in college specifically geared to planning. Instead they came from related fields, including business and accounting. In addition, financial planning can be a second career for professionals such as tax lawyers. Some financial planners previously worked at a management level in banks or businesses; many once worked selling stocks or insurance. Certified public accountants may narrow their practice field and eventually move away from tax accounting into the financial planning field. For example, Ginita Wall is a CPA who developed a financial planning practice that meets the needs of divorced women, a segment of the population that many public accountants do not want to deal with because the situation makes these clients so emotional. Wall entered the field without specifically planning to do so. Cynthia Harrington describes how Wall found a way to shift from accounting to financial planning:

> Wall pursued a piece that she read in the local [San Diego] paper about the top needs of the community. The mayor listed helping women go through a divorce as No. 5. Wall started a Saturday morning support group for divorced women, lectured, authored "150 Ways to Divorce Without Going Broke" [and] became an expert witness and counsel to clients.[36]

In the twenty-first century, more and more colleges are offering training—typically by allowing undergraduates majoring in business administration, finance, or accounting to minor in financial planning. To complete the minor, students take several courses that cover the many different disciplines financial planners must master, including taxation, insurance, and ethics. If college graduates seek training in financial planning, they may enroll in a certificate program (typically about a year long) or a financial planning emphasis within an MBA or Ph.D. program.

An ability to use technology is also essential for planners, and many develop this skill either on their own or through courses. In the twenty-first century more and more planners will find themselves using computers as tools in their practices. They may set up websites that promote their services and allow clients to obtain reports online. E-mail is becoming more and more common as a means of communicating with clients. Experts encourage planners to learn and use this technology to send bulletins and recommendations for action, and to keep in touch with nervous clients when the market is going down. This is because the Internet is fast becoming an essential means of conducting research on a number of issues relevant to planners, including financial trends. However, some planners worry that the information explosion is a double-edged sword. Planner Timothy C. Medley observed:

> Technology also makes a great deal of information available to clients. The threat is that they may begin to ask why they need us. For example, if you use a search engine to find a financial advisor in Mississippi, the first thing that comes up

An Elite Profession?

Financial planners, by and large, deal with clients who are wealthy. This is in part because wealthy people can more easily afford a financial planner's fee and in part because planners who are licensed to sell financial products such as stocks and insurance can make substantial commissions on those products. In What Is Financial Planning, Anyway? *financial planner Trudy Turner expresses her view that she and her professional colleagues should find ways of serving a wider range of clients.*

I do think that middle America is largely being left out [by financial planners], but I am hopeful that will change. I believe we have an obligation to serve a client such as a young professional not far out of college, but what they need is a lot different than what somebody 55 years old needs. Most financial planners at least say they want long-term relationships with clients, and the beauty of it is that these people will become those 55-year-old clients one day. We really have to figure out how to serve this person.

is Financial Engines. This is a firm in California that has a Nobel Prize winner on its staff. You can buy their service for less than 50 bucks a year. We don't have a Nobel Prize winner on our staff.[37]

Even though aspiring financial planners may complete degrees or have other financial experience, many new planners believe that guidance from more seasoned planners is the most valuable training tool. Some financial planning firms have well-organized approaches to training. One young planner, Amy Hoffman, describes her positive experience this way:

I've been lucky enough to work for firms that have provided me a path toward becoming a financial planner. At my current firm, a career path starts with an associate position. The associate learns the ropes, kind of like an old-fashioned apprenticeship. It's a unique situation, and difficult to find, but it's been a very good situation for me.[38]

Certification and Licensing

Financial planning is not a career field that specifically requires a license; however, financial planners may pursue certification to show that they have expertise in the field. One example is the certified financial planner (CFP) designation, which is awarded by the Certified Financial Planner Board of Standards, Inc. To achieve this certification, financial planners must have three to five years of experience, pass an exam, and agree to adhere to the ethical standards set by the board, including agreeing to keep client information confidential. At the core of the ethical rules are mandates that the financial planner act to protect the interests of the client and exercise good judgment when handling clients' affairs. This "fiduciary relationship" between the financial

Young financial planners can obtain invaluable training by working closely with more experienced colleagues.

planner and the client is, according to Charles E. Foster II, "like a tailwind that pushes the financial planner to do what is best for the client. [In other words,] the client comes first and everything else comes second."[39]

In addition to satisfying these criteria to receive the CFP designation, planners must meet educational requirements. Beginning in 2007 these will include a bachelor's degree in any subject and specific training in financial planning. Until then the undergraduate degree is not required, but candidates for certification must show that they have completed coursework in such subjects as risk management and estate planning.

Not all financial planners obtain certification, and those who do have mixed opinions about how much the designation helps them. One planner found that her clients were unfamiliar with certification and therefore were not influenced by that achievement when they decided to hire her. Instead they were persuaded to use her services because of her excellent track record. However, when Eric Rabbanian began his financial planning career, he conducted Internet research to see what measures of skill consumer advocates suggested people look for when hiring a financial planner. What he found convinced him that obtaining the designation was the way to go:

> I did a review of consumer-oriented literature on the Internet, and the advice given to consumers was always, "When you are looking for a financial planner, start with a CFP professional." . . . Now that I'm in business, it strikes me even more that the CFP certification is a necessary step in the field's progression toward a profession. It's similar to an accountant becoming a CPA or a lawyer having to meet bar requirements.[40]

While certification is not required and a specific financial planning license does not exist, financial planners may, because of the activities they engage in, fall within categories that are regulated at either a federal or state level. For example, if planners advise about the worth of stocks or other securities, or suggest whether the client should invest, the state or federal government may require licensing. Selling stocks makes a financial planner subject to the same licensing requirements as stockbrokers.

Too Close for Comfort

Complying with so many different regulations is one of the challenges of the career, and many believe life would be simpler if there were one license and one regulator for their work. Instead planners find themselves dealing with more than one state or federal regulator. Sheryl Garrett, a Kansas-based financial planner, complained: "I could do a $300 project for a client 30 minutes away, across the Kansas-Missouri state line, and I have to get registered there, too. It's the time and the agony of the paperwork, and every state is different. For a small-businessperson trying to do everything right, it can be a real headache."[41]

While technical requirements can inconvenience a financial planner, dealing with the personalities of clients in the highly charged context of personal finance is a challenge that can create more serious headaches. For example, when couples come for appointments, they may use the time to attack each others' spending and other habits, making the planner feel uncomfortably like a marriage counselor. Clients upset about problems outside of the planner's control, such as a downturn in the stock market, sometimes try to place blame on planners, creating conflict that can be stressful. In addition, irate clients may file complaints with regulatory organizations such as the National Association of Securities Dealers, which oversees the behavior of financial planners involved in stockbrokering activities, requiring the planner to spend a significant amount of effort to respond.

A Lucrative and Satisfying Career

Nevertheless, the monetary rewards for those who can juggle the many different demands of the field can be significant. According to surveys conducted by the U.S. Bureau of Labor Statistics, the annual median income for financial planners is $57,700, with the least experienced workers making in the high $20,000 range and the best paid workers making over $145,000 a year.

Besides their pay, financial planners enjoy the personal interactions they have with clients and the feeling that they are partly responsible for an improvement in their clients' lifestyles. When asked for his opinion of the most rewarding part of his career, Rabbanian replied: "Most rewarding in a word: relationships. Relationships with mentors, other planners and clients.

How Financial Planners Are Paid

The Certified Financial Planner Board of Standards, Inc., which oversees the process of certification for financial planners, also provides information to the public. On their website (www.cfp.net) the board explains the many different options for paying financial planners.

There is currently no uniform method by which financial planners are paid. A planner can be paid by a salary paid by the company for which the planner works; by fees based on an hourly rate, a flat rate, or on a percentage of your assets and/or income; by commissions paid by a third party from the products sold to you to carry out the financial planning recommendations; or by a combination of fees and commissions whereby fees are charged for the amount of work done to develop financial planning recommendations [while] commissions are received from any products sold.

Second, being able to educate and make a noticeable difference in the lives of my clients, especially those who are learning that they can actually achieve their goal to be financially independent or provide a great education for their child."[42]

Hoffman shares that enthusiasm: "I remember my grandmother asking me if I liked my job. I told her, 'I love going to work every day. I have fun.' She said that she didn't think she had ever heard anyone in our family say that before."[43]

Chapter 3

Debt Collectors

Debt collectors help creditors, including banks, credit unions, finance companies, and mortgage companies, collect money that people or other businesses owe them. Collectors may work as employees of the business for which they are doing collections (in-house) or in specialized collection companies. They may collect money from individuals (consumer collectors) or from businesses (commercial collectors). Debt collectors perform tasks that lead to the collection of money from people who have failed to pay debts to businesses of all kinds—from video stores to phone companies. Collecting loans, including credit card debts, mortgages, and money borrowed to buy cars, is also a common activity of debt collectors.

As Americans take on more and more loan debt, many of them cannot afford to repay the money they borrow, either because they do not manage their money well, were influenced by the marketing efforts of credit-card companies to take on more debt than they could afford, or because something major changed their lives—for example they divorced or lost a job. Thus, even though borrowers go through screening processes by lenders that include an evaluation of their income and debts and past credit history (whether they have paid other loans on time or have filed for bankruptcy), many end up defaulting (failing to pay according to the terms) on their loans. This trend will increase the demand for debt collectors in the twenty-first century.

Finding and Contacting Debtors

The primary task of debt collectors is to make contact with debtors—people who owe money and are not repaying it in the way they agreed. Collectors typically negotiate with the debtor to determine the amount that will be paid and to set up a schedule for payment. They also keep records of the status of accounts. If they are unable to collect the money, they refer the case to an attorney who will take legal action to recover the debt.

Collectors typically work at desks where they receive computer-generated information from their clients (either their employer if they work for a company that is owed money, or an outside company if they work for a collection agency) about the debtors they will work to collect from. When they receive a new account, collectors must first find the debtor. Not all debtors remain at the address and phone number they originally gave a creditor, and some make themselves deliberately hard to find. Collectors undertake a process called skip tracing to track down people who do not want to be found. They use databases such as electronic white pages that they access online or in CD-ROM form that show addresses and phone numbers of debtors. However, not all of this

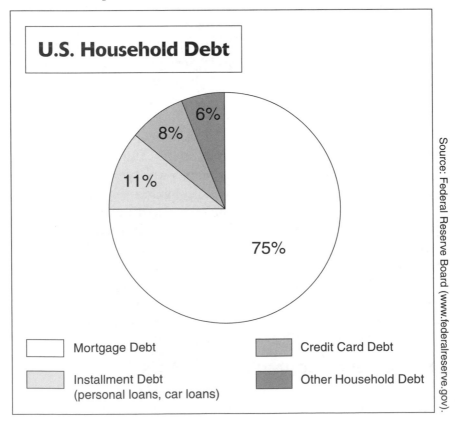

U.S. Household Debt

6%
8%
11%
75%

Mortgage Debt
Installment Debt
(personal loans, car loans)
Credit Card Debt
Other Household Debt

Source: Federal Reserve Board (www.federalreserve.gov).

A Good Career

Claude Organ, an experienced collections manager, explains in an interview with the author why he believes that working as a debt collector can be satisfying.

For somebody who is entrepreneurial and is willing to work hard, [debt collecting] is a tremendous opportunity. Debt collectors can make lots of money [and find satisfaction in the fact that], by and large, part of the compensation is tied to what they collect. Some people enjoy the challenge of negotiating. For them, the thrill is the chase, [the tracking down of] somebody other people have tried to get. There is also "instant gratification" [in debt collecting]; people get a great sense of satisfaction when they collect money and close out a file.

information is current, and debt collectors may also contact neighbors or family members. The post office and phone company are additional resources collectors use to locate debtors.

Once they know where to reach a debtor, collectors make contact, either by calling the debtor or by sending a collection letter. Automation has also replaced the once tedious task of typing collection letters; they can now be automatically generated by the computer. In addition, collectors may use e-mail to send their collection messages. The federal Fair Debt Collection Practices Act, a law that governs collection activities against consumers, requires that written confirmation of a verbal contact be made soon after the verbal notification, and spells out information about the debt that must be presented in any collection letter: "Within five days after you are first contacted, the collector must send you a written notice telling you the amount of money you owe; the name of the creditor to whom you owe the money; and what action to take if you believe you do not owe the money."[44]

Tailoring a Call to the Circumstance

The most common and effective way of reaching debtors is to call them on the telephone. In these conversations collectors use a number of different techniques to negotiate, from pushy to gentle, depending on the situation. Some in the debt-collection business report that the geographic location of the person being called influences how a collector handles the situation. As one commercial collection agency president reported to journalist Brian Leaf, people on the East Coast are approached with a tough attitude while "a softer approach"[45] is used for other regions in the country where people are more likely to be offended by an aggressive conversation.

In addition, when making commercial collections contacts, collectors must be aware of the business relationship between the debtor and the creditor. More often than not the creditor wants to keep the debtor as a customer. When the business being conducted is an especially important part of the creditor's overall business, "there is no way you get on the phone and start screaming,"[46] explains collections executive James Hutchens.

The ultimate goal of the collector also affects his or her technique. In the twenty-first century those goals will evolve because society as a whole is changing. For example, in one significant trend, Americans are living longer and borrowing more money during their lives. And while earlier generations were motivated to pay off debts during their lifetimes, borrowers in the twenty-first century are more likely to owe money even into old age.

As a result of this societal change, a great deal of creditors' money is at stake in probate proceedings. This legal process, which settles a deceased person's financial affairs, differs from state to state. Because of these complexities creditors used to walk away from many of these debts or assign the larger ones to law firms for collection. But some lenders, including credit-card companies such as AT&T Universal Card, are giving these cases to in-house collectors who specialize in probate. Not only must these collectors learn the legal process of probate, they must also be adept at handling people who are understandably distraught at the loss of a loved one. Leslie J. Gartin, assistant vice president of the probate department at AT&T Universal Card, explains the tension between collecting and sympathizing: "[In probate collections] you are often dealing with people that have been left helter-skelter. You want to make sure they are being treated properly. . . . [At the same time, we] don't care why [a person] died; he [or she] still owes us money."[47] Thus, collectors may listen a bit to surviving spouses who express grief, but will then quickly turn the conversation to the subject at hand—the payment of the debt.

Tracking Accounts

Collectors use computers in all phases of their work. For example, they use them to access accounts. This saves an enormous amount of time because collectors do not have to produce paper reports, make and file copies of them, and see that they are mailed. Instead they use online systems that allow daily contact without the hassles, such as missed calls associated with phone communications. Journalist J.W. Dysart reports on the function of one computer system used by a commercial collection company: "[According to Credit Systems company president Harry B. Keen] the system allows clients to list accounts, report payments, place accounts on hold, and cancel accounts, as well as communicate with the collector regarding an individual account."[48] Collectors using systems such as these access them throughout the day to find out if there are accounts they should no longer try to collect because the debtor has indicated no willingness to comply and legal action will be commenced, or because some portion of the money due has been paid.

A debt collector uses a predictive dialer and a headset to contact a debtor.

In addition to typical computers, collectors use predictive dialers, machines that are part computer and part telephone. Predictive dialers are programmed with thousands of debtor telephone numbers. Those numbers are called automatically and, on the most advanced dialer machines, a collector is signaled when a person rather than an answering machine has picked up the line. The predictive dialer can be an important tool because it shows the details about the account being collected as it initiates the phone call. Thus collectors do not waste time searching through index cards or files for the information they need once they reach the debtor. These systems are being enhanced to perform other helpful functions. For example, collectors can access information about previous calls they have made to a debtor to find out the best times to reach that debtor by phone.

While machines that dial automatically can dramatically increase the number of calls collectors make in a day, technology alone does not guarantee that collectors will do a better job. Industry expert Orville D. Young cautions: "Too many operations in the industry use power dialers as a panacea. You cannot use technology alone. It has to be in concert with management and training."[49] For example, collectors must be trained to leave legally proper and effective messages when the dialers get through to machines or to people in the household other than the debtor.

Wanted: Collectors Who Can Sell

Collectors in the twenty-first century need better interpersonal skills than ever before because they are increasingly called upon to tackle difficult circumstances, such as collecting from a deceased person's estate. In addition, they are becoming an integral part of company programs that find ways to keep debtors as customers. Collectors will be most in demand if they can walk a fine line between pushing for a payment and selling a company's other financial products, such as a new loan that consolidates other loans. Journalist Trevor Curwin describes one such program implemented at The Credit Store, a company that buys debts from businesses that have been unsuccessful at collecting these amounts themselves:

> [The Credit Store] tracks down the debtors and negotiates how much of the consumer's outstanding debt will be paid and how much will remain. The debtor is then offered a credit card from a . . . bank [that is a partner to The Credit

Store]. . . . [The new credit card has a] balance equal to, or slightly [higher] than, the outstanding balance of the bad debt.[50]

Other major creditors are using a similar approach. At Bank of America collectors are called "financial counselors" because their work involves so much more than the traditional work of collectors. One senior vice president of the bank, Michael O. Radesky, explains that he is not interested in hiring "people with collections training. . . . In most cases, I wish that customers didn't know they [were] talking to a collector."[51] Instead Radesky wants people who have the ability to get the debt paid and keep the debtor as a customer who will use the bank's other services.

Persuasion is a big part of the collector's job, and the ability to get one's point across while getting to know what is truly going on with a debtor is an absolute must for success. For example, a collector may have to keep repeating that money is owed but at the same time be listening for things the debtor says that give clues about how much of the debt can be paid and when. If the debtor mentions getting a tax refund, then the collector will follow up and ask when it is expected and how much of the refund can go toward paying the debt. Typically collectors do not settle for the debtor's first offer. Instead they push the debtor to agree to more. This kind of debtor contact requires more skill than most people realize. Journalist Burney Simpson interviewed collection executive Michael A. DiMarco and summarized his opinion of the qualities of top-notch collectors this way: "What counts is the ability to listen, to negotiate, to convince, and to have the thick skin required to take the occasional insult or slammed phone."[52]

Collectors must also have the ability to follow company procedures and legal rules. For example, collectors who work in independent agencies must comply with the federal Fair Debt Collection Practices Act. The act outlines activities of debt collectors that are not allowed. These include, for instance: "The use or threat of use of violence or other criminal means to harm the physical person, reputation, or property of any person [and] the use of obscene or profane language or language the natural consequence of which is to abuse the hearer or reader." Collectors are also prohibited from "causing a telephone to ring or engaging any

Legal Compliance

Collectors in agencies must comply with the terms of the federal Fair Debt Collection Practices Act. The act is enforced by the Federal Trade Commission. This excerpt from the commission's website (www.ftc.gov) summarizes some of the restrictions on debt collectors.

A collector may contact you in person, by mail, telephone, telegram, or fax. However, a debt collector may not contact you at inconvenient times or places, such as before 8 a.m. or after 9 p.m., unless you agree. A debt collector also may not contact you at work if the collector knows that your employer disapproves of such contacts. . . . You can stop a debt collector from contacting you by writing a letter to the collector telling them to stop. Once the collector receives your letter, they may not contact you again except to say there will be no further contact or to notify you that the debt collector or the creditor intends to take some specific action. Please note, however, that sending such a letter to a collector does not make the debt go away if you actually owe it. You could still be sued by the debt collector or your original creditor.

person in telephone conversation repeatedly or continuously with intent to annoy, abuse, or harass any person at the called number."[53] The best collectors understand these laws, know their limits, and can make good judgments about how to maximize their effectiveness within those limits.

Collectors acquire their skills through on-the-job training. Thus they typically begin in this career as a high school graduate. However, collectors with some college courses will be highly desirable in the twenty-first century because of the increasingly complex demands of the collections setting. Post–high school coursework in communications, business, or computers will make candidates for these positions especially appealing.

People Do Not Like Collectors

Collectors face many challenges, not the least of which is the negative reaction of debtors who do not wish to be asked for payments that they cannot afford to make. A debtor may slam down the phone when a collector calls, but the most unpleasant encounters are those that occur in person. While personal contact is less frequent than in the past because collectors have so many other ways to reach people (by phone or e-mail, for example), collectors may go to a debtor's home under certain circumstances. Examples include cases in which the debtor's phone is not working or in which the collector is unsure about personal information, such as an address. In addition, although it is more typical to involve lawyers to bring legal action at this later stage, collectors may go to a person's home to retrieve items that were bought or rented in exchange for a debtor's broken promise to make payments (typically monthly payments over a period of time).

In one in-person collection attempt gone awry, a collector asked a debtor to surrender a car. When he arrived at the debtor's place, the car was in the driveway—in pieces. In another case, John E. Metz, who now runs his own collection agency, attempted

Debtors like this couple who determine they are unable to afford their payments often react in a negative fashion toward collectors.

to pick up furniture. The debtor, who had just been evicted (removed from his house for not paying rent), was in a very bad mood. As Metz describes the situation, "When we went out to get the furniture, [the person who owed the money] had some kind of sword that he was waving, threatening to kill me. I said, 'Hey, it's furniture. It's not that big a deal' [then] the police took him away."[54]

Limited Advancement

Aside from being unpopular as a group, collectors find that they typically have fewer advancement opportunities than others in finance jobs. Thus turnover is rampant among collectors, in some industries reaching 100 percent (meaning that by the end of one year, none of the same employees who started in the job are still there). This turnover is partly due to the nature of collecting—people tire of the negative responses they receive when they make contact with debtors—and to the fact that the pay for the typical collector is quite low.

In 2001 the median annual income for collectors was twenty-six thousand dollars, with the highest-paid collectors making about forty thousand dollars or more and the lowest making eighteen thousand dollars or less. The most experienced collectors, who work with debts that have been outstanding the longest, had median incomes of about fifty thousand dollars a year. In rare cases outstanding collectors can earn over one hundred thousand dollars a year. According to one 1998 study, collection managers made, as an average, about sixty-seven thousand dollars a year. Collectors may be paid a straight salary or a combination of salary and commission.

Because turnover is expensive for employers who have to constantly retrain workers, companies are experimenting with incentive programs that make these jobs more appealing in the long run. They may beef up popular benefits such as company-sponsored health- and life-insurance programs. They may also agree to pay employees back for education tuition. Some managers offer "perks" such as food or gifts to employees who perform well.

Finding Ways to Grow

Limited advancement opportunity is another aspect of collections jobs that many feel is a negative. Nevertheless, experienced collectors typically have the option of working the more difficult accounts—those that have been unpaid for the longest time or those in probate, for instance—or advancing to supervisory positions. Supervisors have the responsibility to keep watch over collectors in their department to make sure they are meeting company goals for recovering money owed and that they are complying with company procedures as well as federal and state laws. Supervisors also oversee scheduling of work hours and will counsel employees who have problems, such as consistent tardiness. They also participate in on-the-job training of less-experienced employees.

Companies are also increasing the amount of effort they put into training their collectors in an effort to increase professionalism and to give employees a sense that they have a way to grow within the company. Because consumer debt is expected to grow significantly, attracting excellent workers will become more critical than ever in the twenty-first century. In addition to teaching skills closely related to their employees' work, companies may stimulate employees by training them in general business skills such as management. Human resources executive Peter A. Pugal

A Cause of Burnout?

Debt collectors use predictive dialers to help them make dozens of calls each day. These machines combine the capabilities of a telephone and a computer. They automatically dial numbers that have been programmed into them to reach debtors who owe money. The dialers can alert a collector when a real person answers the phone and can create a history that allows the collector to call back at times of the day when the call has been successfully placed before. However, some collection managers worry that the dialers can lead to burnout because they push the collector to keep a steady, often fast, pace throughout the workday. Also, while statistically speaking more calls placed means more personal contacts made, collectors may feel pressured to increase the quantity, rather than the quality, of their contacts.

believes this makes good sense in an environment that will require more and more skill from collectors. "The collections industry is becoming increasingly complex, and we want to educate our employees to keep up with these changes."[55]

Collectors may start their own business as a way of developing professionally and radically improving their compensation. Now head of a company that in 1999 worked two hundred thousand debt-collection cases at a time, Alvin D. Rice started on his own after his services were no longer needed at a big company. Journalist F. Romall Smalls reports how Rice began as an entrepreneur: "Armed with just $100 and his experience in the field, Rice, 38, started in the basement of his home, becoming one of the few African Americans in the country to own a debt collections company."[56]

While collections work is not necessarily a lifelong occupation, more employers are attempting to define it as a career. Pugal describes his company's efforts this way: "Turnover is a major problem in this industry. We're working to reverse that trend by creating more attractive employment opportunities, using the best practices and principles we have observed in other industries."[57]

Chapter 4

Stockbrokers

Stockbrokers help people use their money to try to make more money. This is called investing. Stockbrokers help their clients invest in a variety of different types of financial instruments, but they are called stockbrokers because stocks are a common investment they buy and sell for clients (investors). Investors who buy a share of stock are buying a part of a company. Companies benefit because, in exchange for these shares of stock, they receive investors' money, which allows them to pay for operating expenses. Investors who buy stock hope to benefit from increases in the value of the stock. If a company does well, its stock becomes worth more over time, increasing the value of the stockholders' shares.

Shares of stock are bought and sold through "markets," such as the New York Stock Exchange (NYSE), if the stocks meet an exchange's requirements, or "over the counter," a computer and phone network for selling stocks, if they do not meet stability and size requirements for exchange trading. Stockbrokers act as intermediaries between their clients and those who wish to either buy or sell in response to the client's order. If the stock in question is listed on an exchange, the actual buying and selling takes place there through floor brokers and specialists with whom the stockbroker places an order electronically. For over-the-counter stocks, stockbrokers enlist the services of traders who deal directly with other traders.

In addition to implementing the purchase and sale of stock and other investments, stockbrokers advise their clients on the best ways to manage their investments, and keep in touch with them about trends in financial markets and new opportunities for investment. Stockbrokers help with other kinds of investments, for instance buying bonds (a financial instrument through which investors loan money to government organizations or companies, receiving interest and the loaned money back on a set date) and mutual funds, in which many investors pool their money so they

A Hectic but Controlled Trading Environment

The New York Stock Exchange is the largest securities exchange in the United States. It was founded in 1792 by twenty-four brokers and is now located in a New York City building that dates back to 1903. The NYSE website (www.nyse.com) describes how what seems like a hectic environment is really one that adds stability to financial markets and the economy.

A first-time visitor to the NYSE may be easily baffled by the hectic activity involved in the buying and selling of stock. The trading floor resembles a beehive of activity where market professionals cluster around computer screens calling out buy and sell orders. In addition to the main room of the trading floor, where the opening and closing bell is rung, four other trading rooms comprise a total of 48,000 square feet. While the trading floor may be a hectic place, the activity is closely monitored to maintain a fair and orderly market. The NYSE is governed by a precise set of rules and regulations that ensure smooth and efficient trading of billions of shares of stock every day.

Traders are busy at work in the hectic environment of the New York Stock Exchange.

can take advantage of the skills of professional fund managers who invest in a diverse range of investments.

Stockbrokers are first and foremost salespeople because they must convince clients to use their services and to buy their financial products. Some stockbrokers sell their services and products to individual investors (retail brokering), while others sell to large companies, such as banks and pension funds that manage retirement savings (institutional brokering). Stockbrokers work in large and small brokerage firms, which may be part of larger financial institutions such as commercial banks or investment banks. Increasingly, stockbrokers work for discount and online brokerage firms, which handle trades but give little investment advice.

Research to Benefit Clients

Stockbrokers are valuable to their clients because they can find and understand the significance of the vast amounts of information that help investors make informed decisions. Thus one of the key tasks of stockbrokers is to keep abreast of financial information. Stockbrokers spend a significant amount of time each day gathering this information from many sources to help create pictures of what has happened, and to form opinions about what will happen, in the economy, financial markets, specific industries, and individual companies. For instance, a stockbroker notices whether changes in government regulations will improve the value of companies subject to the regulations.

Sources include companies themselves, which issue annual reports and other information that shows how profitable they expect to be. Journals, newspapers, and online databases provide charts, stock prices, and information about management changes in companies and the development of new technologies that can affect the value of a company. Well-known journals include *Barron's*, the *Wall Street Journal*, and *Investor's Business Daily*. Websites abound that give information showing how companies stack up to other companies within the industry, track stock trends, and provide commentary and advice about the economy. Stockbrokers also use Bloomberg machines, which are self-contained computers that give real-time stock quotes and a wealth of other financial information. One famous stockbroker, Andrew A. Lanyi, describes how technological developments in the late twentieth century forever changed the way stockbrokers do business:

> When I started my career, one of the old-timers let the paper-tape run through his fingers and wrote the current prices of some of our favorite stocks on a blackboard. Today, I have five computer screens facing me—and four more confronting my two assistants. The screens supply us with [stock] price quotes, news, history of customer contacts, charts, and sales and earnings reports—and whole portfolios that are analyzed in a number of different ways.[58]

The *Summary of Commentary on Current Economic Conditions*, commonly called the Beige Book, is published by the Federal Reserve Board and is another useful source that stockbrokers use to get a sense of economic trends and events that could affect

A stockbroker researches stock prices and quotes in order to provide his clients with sound investment advice.

their clients' portfolios. This report is published eight times each year and is based on information collected through the Federal Reserve Bank's twelve districts (regions of the country). Each district compiles information that it obtains by talking with businesses about many factors. These include how well their products are selling, what their plans are for production, and whether they expect to close manufacturing facilities or open new ones. The district reports also include information from other sources, including consultants and experts on economic issues and market trends. This example of a paragraph from the July 2003 Beige Book shows how a stockbroker can use this resource to look for signs of future successes or problems for clients who own stock in companies that sell information technology, vehicles, weapons, and materials used to build houses:

> [The Chicago district's] report noted that nationwide light vehicle production was "pretty good" through mid-July and that heavy equipment orders edged up, in part because of a weaker dollar. San Francisco reported that new orders in the information technology sector strengthened, reducing inventory levels. Suppliers to the defense and military industry in the Cleveland and Atlanta districts continued to report strong orders, while Boston and Dallas noted a pickup in demand for personal computers and computer hardware. Philadelphia added that demand increased for residential construction materials and orders rose for printing and industrial machinery components.[59]

Many stockbrokers rely heavily on the reports of their firm's research department, which employs analysts who become experts in, for instance, specific industries. Stockbrokers receive information from their research departments in written form (through reports furnished in hard copy or by the firm's intranet) or at meetings. Carine de Boissezon, an equities saleswoman (stockbroker), describes how stockbrokers can benefit from meetings with their firms' analysts: "The research analysts . . . give talks about key propriety research, [financial] results that have just come out, or any other idea that can help our clients with their investment decisions."[60]

Setting and Implementing Client Goals

Stockbrokers use the information they gather to advise clients how to best meet their financial goals, whether to take risks to try to make a big profit in the immediate future or to stay in the stock market long-term and attempt to make a steady but more modest gain. Stockbrokers discuss with their clients about how much risk the client is willing to take to aim for a higher return (profit) on the money invested, then develop an investment portfolio consistent with this decision. Stockbrokers cannot control the many forces—from the general economy to political and world events to the U.S. Food and Drug Administration rulings on a drug company's products—that affect how investments perform. Therefore they must work hard to develop strategies that hedge against such events.

One of the most common approaches to solving the problem of unpredictability is for a stockbroker to develop a balanced portfolio; that is, a collection of investments that includes some that are conservative and some that are risky. Such a portfolio would also include investments that do not all have a tendency to react to the same events. For instance, a portfolio that had nothing but stock in companies that make missiles and other weapons could fail dramatically in times of extended peace or if Congress decided to cut military spending. One well-known investment expert, John C. Bogle, explains how stockbrokers can help clients interested in staying in the stock market for the long haul develop successful and balanced portfolios:

> [Stockbrokers] can be helpful to investors who make decisions about buying individual stocks by helping them put those decisions into the proper portfolio context. Of course, an individual would have to be diversified enough [have enough variety] in his or her own portfolio to gain that advantage. Brokers can help select a range of stocks for investors, so a portfolio doesn't consist of all large, all small, or all tech stocks.[61]

Over time many successful stockbrokers develop strategies that they use for most, if not all, of their clients. They may, for example, look for stocks that have been proven over a number of years or that are in companies that satisfy basic needs, such as providing medical care or selling fast food. One stockbroker, Mark Dick, used the psychology he studied in graduate school to decide on an approach that has made him so popular with clients that they send their adult children and grandchildren to him. His strategy is based on what he learned about human nature—that people are more emotionally affected by losing at something than by winning. Thus, he reasons, clients are more likely to be satisfied by long-term investment strategies that keep their money growing rather than short-term strategies that have the potential to reap quick profits but can turn sour. By investing in conservative stocks, Dick believes he gives investors an incentive to stay in the stock market and, just as important, to keep coming back to him for advice. As he puts it: "When an investor is starting out, the worst thing that can happen is to lose money. It's like if you were to touch a hot stove. You'd pull back. If you begin investing

An Exceptional Effort

Stockbrokers often make recommendations to their clients about which stocks to purchase and which to sell based on research reports received from professionals who specialize in analyzing stocks. However, one well-known stockbroker believes that he and his colleagues can do far more for clients besides making quick suggestions based on someone else's research. In his book, Confessions of a Stockbroker, *Andrew A. Lanyi gives an example of the kind of exceptional effort a stockbroker can make for a client.*

Too frequently you get an excited pitch [from your broker] to buy, then no follow-up, until the broker decides it's time for another commission and calls you to recommend a sale. . . . [You may be tempted to sell a stock that has increased in value in order to cash in on your profit.] If you have a good broker and he does his homework, he just may call you and say: "Charlie, I talked today to the chairman of the company, talked to their biggest supplier, talked to their biggest customer—and business is far better than we expected. In fact, the figures are terrific. My suggestion is that you shouldn't take a profit on your 3,000 shares. Instead, you should buy 2,000 more!"

A broker discusses investment options with his clients. With experience, brokers develop effective investment strategies to share with their clients.

with $30,000, and your very first statement says your account is down to $23,000, you're going to be unhappy and put all your money in the bank the next week."[62]

While stockbrokers give their clients advice, the clients themselves are ultimately responsible for making investment decisions. Thus stockbrokers spend many stressful hours reacting with speed and accuracy to instructions from their clients to buy or sell stocks. Executing a trade on time is extremely important because the prices of shares of stock fluctuate constantly, and if a stockbroker delays executing a buy or sell order, the client can suffer huge losses. The way the trade is executed is also decided by the client and must be strictly followed by the stockbroker. For example, the client may wish to place a market order, which is a request to buy or sell the stock at the best price available at the time the order is placed. However, if a client wants to wait to see if the stock reaches a certain price before buying or selling, he or she will place a limit order, which instructs the stockbroker to do nothing unless the target price is reached. This type of order is further complicated because the client specifies the amount of time he or she wants the order to stay open, which can be anywhere from a day or until the client cancels it.

Stockbrokers implement the purchase or sale of stock either by notifying the firm's stock traders of the transaction (for over-the-counter stocks) or by placing the order electronically with an exchange. The orders are handled by floor traders and specialists who work on the floor of the stock exchange. The way specialists handle a trade is described by the New York Stock Exchange on its website:

> Each stock is allocated to a specialist, who acts as an auctioneer in specific stocks at a designated location. All buying and selling of a stock occurs at that location, called a trading post. . . . The people who gather around the specialist's post are referred to as the trading crowd. Bids to buy and offers to sell are spoken aloud so that anyone present has an opportunity to participate in the buying and selling. This enhances the competitive determination of prices. When the highest bid meets the lowest offer, a trade is executed.[63]

NYSE floor traders and specialists act like auctioneers and bid for the best stock prices.

After the purchase or sale is made, the specialist sends confirmation electronically to the accounts of the buyers and sellers and to a central data source (a consolidated tape) that broadcasts the transaction worldwide. The broker handling the transaction lets the clients know the final price and makes sure that written confirmation is sent right away. (Many of these tasks are handled by the stockbroker's assistant or through automation.) Both the seller and buyer settle the transaction within three business days, meaning that if stock has been purchased, the buyer deposits the price in his or her brokerage account. For the seller, proceeds of the sale are deposited in the account. Both the buyer and the seller also pay commissions to the stockbroker at this point.

Selling Themselves

While stockbrokers must be good advisers and know the markets, their most critical skill is the ability to sell themselves, because unless they have clients they cannot survive. Finding clients who want to use their services takes a significant amount of time in the beginning. Stockbrokers find prospects (possible future clients) by buying marketing lists of people with certain characteristics (those who own expensive cars or subscribe to financial magazines, for instance) or by placing ads. They also select people from the phone book. They call people out of the blue (cold calls), introduce themselves to the person who answers the phone, and try to find a way to keep the person interested long enough to let them know that the stockbroker has something to offer. Often stockbrokers will say that they have an exciting tip about a stock that research shows is likely to go up.

While being a consistent cold caller who could close a stock transaction (get the person to agree to a purchase) was once the most valuable skill for stockbrokers, many observers see a need for stockbrokers of the twenty-first century to develop more expertise as financial consultants. This is the result not only of competition from online brokerage firms but also because the current and upcoming generations of investors (baby boomers and gen-xers) tend to be more skeptical of salespeople than their parents or grandparents were. They understand that making commissions on stocks rather than seeing to the overall financial needs of a client may create conflicts that could lead to a stockbroker's looking out for his or her own interests—making money—instead of the client's. Harry Dent, a well-known author and investment consultant, cautions that the tried and true ways of succeeding as a stockbroker may soon be a thing of the past. His advice to future stockbrokers is to change with the times:

> If I were established and really providing my clients with the unbiased help they need, I wouldn't be worried about the future. But if I were starting out, I certainly wouldn't want to cold call and try to sell someone a product over the phone. I would try to develop skills and then demonstrate those skills through seminars, for example, so the right kinds of [prospective customers] could get to know me.[64]

Stockbrokers of the twenty-first century will continue to wrestle with the rise of technology. Computers and the Internet allow investors to make trades online for a fraction of the cost of a stockbroker's traditional commission. These bargain online services do not provide counseling, but many people are comfortable using them any way; while executing a trade for $10 means that online investors do not get the benefit of a stockbroker's experience, it seems appealing to many people who also use the Internet to research investment information, including details about companies and economic trends. Elizabeth Sikorovsky, who consults on electronic commerce, believes that the rise of Internet investing means that stockbrokers will have to come up with new ways of serving clients. "High priced commissions are going quickly. It's very hard to convince a customer now that a simple transaction is worth $300. The winners are going to be players who offer their customers high service and low, if not free, trading commissions."[65]

This trend is forcing many stockbrokers to look long and hard at how they can be of value to potential customers. They are attempting to respond to the question posed by many potential clients: If I can take care of trading on my own, why do I need a stockbroker? One solution is to broaden the type of advice stockbrokers give to clients. Thus many stockbrokers are expected to perform more like financial planners, giving advice that touches on all the financial needs of clients, from life insurance coverage to college savings.

A news program reports stock information. The widespread availability of stock information enables many investors to trade without a broker's help.

Because stockbrokers will spend more time on this type of counseling, they will have to find ways of earning money beyond the old way of charging commissions on trades. Charging a fee for the overall service of financial consulting is considered by many to be the wave of the future. Some stockbrokers may charge a percentage of the value of the portfolio. Merrill Lynch, one of the largest brokerage firms, is responding to both of these problems— the loss of interest in a stockbroker's advice and the growing reluctance to pay large commissions—by finding ways to stay valuable to its customers. Consultant John Payne describes the firm's efforts this way: "In order to [keep themselves valuable in the eyes of clients], Merrill Lynch is saying to its retail clients, let's move you to a fee-based model, with unlimited trading for $1500/year, and access to varying levels of advice and guidance. They are seeking to change how the consumer perceives them as a financial consultant."[66]

Staying Within the Law

Although stockbrokers must be good salespeople, because they work in an environment that is highly regulated they must have the integrity and good judgment to comply with weighty legal and ethical responsibilities—even at the expense of a sale. Two important regulatory agencies in the United States are the Securities and Exchange Commission (SEC) and the National Association of Securities Dealers (NASD). The SEC is a federal agency that oversees compliance with securities laws. The NASD is a professional organization that sets and enforces practice guidelines for stockbrokers. The SEC has the enforcement power to ensure that companies make full disclosure to the public about their financial information so that investment decisions can be made wisely. On its website the commission explains how it also becomes involved in the regulation of stockbrokers:

> The SEC also oversees other key participants in the securities world [besides companies], including stock exchanges, broker-dealers [stockbrokers], investment advisors, mutual funds, and public utility holding companies. Here again, the SEC is concerned primarily with promoting disclosure of important information, enforcing the securities laws, and protecting investors who interact with these various organizations and individuals.[67]

All brokerage firms must, according to federal law, become members of the NASD, which has the authority to make sure that the firms and the stockbrokers who work there do not take advantage of clients or otherwise violate rules of fair practice. The regulations are extensive and the NASD has the power to discipline those who violate them by imposing fines, and suspending or barring them from working as stockbrokers. The NASD website lists many different kinds of conduct that are prohibited. These include:

> Recommending to a customer the purchase or sale of a security that is unsuitable given the customer's age, financial situation, investment objective, and investment experience. . . . Misrepresenting or failing to disclose material facts concerning an investment. Examples of information that may be considered material and that should be accurately presented to customers include: the risks of investing in a particular security; the charges or fees involved; company financial

information; and technical or analytical information, such as bond ratings. . . . Removing funds or securities from a customer's account without the customer's prior authorization.[68]

The Stress of Exams and Changing Markets

Because the public has so much at stake in the way stockbrokers conduct business, states regulate who may do this job through an extensive process that begins after the stockbroker has completed an undergraduate degree (usually in finance or business) and on-the-job training. This training may be informal or through a structured program at the brokerage firm or financial institution where stockbrokers work. The next step is to obtain licensing in the state where they work and then to register as representatives of their firms. This process requires them to pass an examination given by the NASD and to have at least four months' experience working for a firm that is registered with the NASD. A second exam is required by most states and, as stockbrokers expand their services to be more like financial planners, they make themselves subject to additional regulations that apply to planners.

While the exams are highly stressful, the most negative aspect of these jobs stems from the nature of the stockbrokers' products. Stocks and other investments are volatile—their prices change quickly—and they and the market as a whole can go quickly into a slump. Thus stockbrokers must work hard and fast and must daily face the reality that they can lose a great deal of money for their clients. Their success and the success of the institutions that employ them are linked to the well-being of the economy and the stock market, which can never be guaranteed. When the stock market is going up (a bull market), stockbrokers can be highly successful and make a great deal of money. If the stock market is tending down (a bear market), stockbrokers are apt to lose clients and jobs.

Counterbalancing the lack of job security is the potential to make a great deal of money. Stockbrokers typically begin by earning a small annual salary (a couple of thousand dollars a month) or a draw against commissions, meaning that the brokerage firm makes up the difference between the commissions earned and an agreed-upon monthly salary. Thus, if the stockbroker were to receive $2000 a month and in January earned $400 in commis-

Stockbrokers Deal with Rejection

Stockbrokers must market themselves, often by "cold calling" hundreds of people a day. In Women in Finance, *stockbroker Kathleen Piaggesi tells how she copes with the rejection that inevitably comes when a salesperson calls people who have not previously requested the contact.*

The ability to ignore being ignored was my biggest asset when I first started. You have to be able to call people knowing that they don't want to talk to you, and continue to call in a positive professional way. Then when you're not able to convince them after trying earnestly that you have something that they should be interested in or at least listen to, you have to be able to walk away from it. [To make a sale you] start with your product, a research report or a service that looks at the market or a particular stock or group of stocks in a certain way. Then a client may say, "I'm interested. I'd like to pay you and see more."

sions, the firm would contribute $1600 to make up the difference between that and $2000. The amount contributed by the firm varies from month to month because the commissions vary. Stockbrokers are eventually paid on a commission-only basis. The U.S. Bureau of Labor Statistics reports that in 2000 the median earnings for stockbrokers was about $56,000, with the lowest earnings in the middle $20,000 range (most likely beginning stockbrokers) and the highest earnings in the $145,000 range and up. In the twenty-first century, more stockbrokers will receive salaries and bonuses because more will work for discount and online brokerage firms which do not generate enough in commissions to provide adequate compensation. This trend, along with the changing needs and expectations of potential clients, will challenge stockbrokers and lead to success for those who enjoy working on the edge and changing with the times.

Chapter 5

Tellers and Customer Service Representatives

Customer service representatives (CSRs) and tellers at financial institutions such as banks and credit unions handle customer contacts for their employers. They implement everyday transactions such as depositing checks and balancing the cash in their cash drawers (tellers) and opening new accounts and taking loan applications (CSRs). While bank customers once conducted business primarily with tellers (who typically handle transactions that are more routine), the teller window will soon become the least likely place for customers to have face-to-face or voice-to-voice contact with financial institution representatives. Instead, many teller services are expected to be taken over by CSRs, not only in branches but also at call centers where the CSRs will "partner" with technology to provide services traditionally handled by tellers and also to market new services to customers. These services will help to smooth the way for customers using computers, voice-activated phone systems, and automated teller machines.

Taking Care of Business

Although in-person banking is becoming less common, CSRs and tellers still work in bank or credit union branches. They have a number of duties that help the normal day-to-day operations of the institutions flow smoothly. These tasks may assist or overlap with tellers or other employees in the branch, such as loan officers. For example, the CSR may help a customer fill out a loan application or obtain a credit report to facilitate the loan application process. When a customer opens a new account, the CSR gives the money or check for deposit to a teller for processing.

Opening a checking account is a typical duty for a CSR working in a bank branch. CSRs greet customers who wish to establish a banking relationship and recommend different options for the checking account. Depending on how much money the customer wishes to deposit, these services may range from a simple student account—for which banks often waive fees, even if only a small amount of money is deposited—to money-market accounts for customers who have a significant amount of money to deposit and who want to earn as much money on their bank accounts as possible.

Once the customer agrees to the type of account, the CSR finds out the exact amount and the form (cash or check) of the initial deposit. The CSR uses a computer terminal to enter required information, such as the customer's address and the names of others on the account, and obtains samples of the signatures of those who will use the account. The CSR also offers services that are related to the checking account; for example what style of check the customer wishes to use (one with pretty pictures or one that is plain).

Once the account has been set up, the CSR gives the deposit to the teller. The teller counts the money and adds up any checks that are part of the deposit and compares them with the amounts noted on the deposit slip—the record of the transaction filled out by the customer or the CSR. The teller then makes a computer entry to show that the money is being put into the customer's account. The teller provides the customer with a receipt that is often generated automatically by the computer and puts the money and checks in the cash drawer to reconcile later.

Part of the Marketing Team

CSRs, and increasingly tellers, also sell services such as auto loans or investment devices such as individual retirement accounts (IRAs). Once they find that a customer is interested in a new

A Blend of Teller and Customer Service Skills

In the twenty-first century, tellers are expected to become far less visible in traditional settings such as bank branches and will be expected to develop customer service skills to remain marketable. This selection from the Occupational Outlook Handbook *further explains this trend.*

Even though some banks have streamlined their branches, the total number of bank branches is expected to increase to meet the needs of a growing population. Branches are being added in nontraditional locations, such as grocery stores, malls, and mobile trailers designed to reach people who do not have easy access to banks. Often, these branches are open longer hours and offer greater customer convenience. Many of these non-traditional branch offices are small and are staffed by tellers who also have customer service training. As a result, tellers who can provide a variety of financial services will be in greater demand in the future.

To remain marketable, bank tellers like this woman must develop excellent customer service skills.

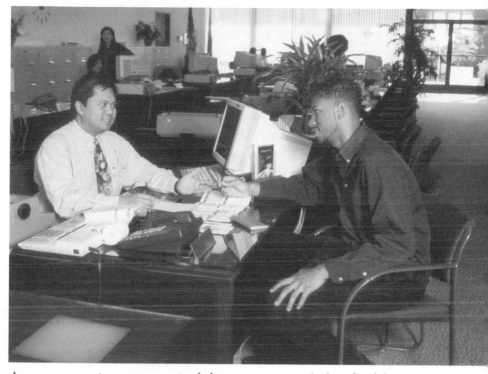

A customer service representative helps a customer apply for a bank loan. CSRs aggressively sell bank services such as loans.

service, CSRs may implement the service themselves or refer the customer to another employee who is an expert in that service, such as a financial consultant for a customer who is interested in advice on how to manage and invest money.

Sales as a component of customer service is a recent development. It became common after new laws were passed in the late twentieth century that allowed banks to sell a wider variety of financial products than they could before. A study of work habits and wages published in 2003 outlines what this means on a day-to-day basis for CSRs:

> As retail financial services diversified and grew more competitive, banks added sales activities to CSRs' jobs. These sales efforts required CSRs to refer customers to product specialists, as well as to "cross-sell" to existing customers (by convincing them to buy additional products and services). In the 1990s, banks extended CSRs' responsibilities even more broadly, asking them to sell more complex products such as

mutual funds, and developed new [information technology] systems to support both service and sales activities.[69]

Computers Guide Customer Relations

Financial institutions are increasingly using computer technology to assist CSRs in their marketing efforts and to guide CSRs in fine-tuning customer interactions. For instance, institutions are adding notations to account information computer screens that remind the CSR to ask if a customer needs additional services, such as a home equity loan or investment advice. The most sophisticated computer systems pull together the information about a customer and make a decision about the most appropriate products. For example, a CSR would be prompted to offer investment services to a customer with a large savings account.

CSRs are also expected to understand and sell the use of company technology to their customers. Understanding a product is not the only key to successfully redirecting customers to technology. Finding a tactful way to tell a customer in essence not to bother you again can be a bit of a challenge. Executive Parrish Arturi suggests: "When someone calls to ask for a copy of a check, the banker can say, 'Did you know you can get this online?'"[70] They are also expected to encourage customers to use voice recognition phone systems instead of dialing through to talk with a live person.

CSRs use computers to handle many tasks such as entering or editing information about account holders and opening or closing bank accounts. CSRs also use computers as tools to define the nature of their relationships with customers. By electronically compiling information about the customers' banking habits and how much money they have invested in the institution or borrowed from it, databases assign ratings to customers that show the CSR how important their business is to the institution. CSRs then follow company policy about how to deal with each customer in light of these ratings. John J. Lafkas and Larry W. Hunter describe how one of these systems works:

> The system featured a small box in the corner of the customer's account screen (visible to, but rarely noticed by, the customer) that contained either an X, an N, or a $. Managers

instructed employees to treat "$" customers with the utmost courtesy, while "X" patrons were unlikely to receive friendly responses to complaints or requests for fee waivers.[71]

A New Environment

In addition to technological changes, the physical setting of the CSR and teller workplace is changing. There will be far fewer bank branches in the twenty-first century, and some will exist in unusual settings such as grocery stores. This change will also lead to a merger of the job duties of CSRs and tellers because small staffs make broad job skills critical. For instance, previously a CSR would open a new account and give the deposit to the teller, but now the whole process is being handled by one person designated as a CSR. The Bank of Smithtown, New York, uses furniture to set a welcoming, flexible atmosphere that allows for a seamless transition between CSR and teller functions. For conferencing with customers, CSRs sit at a P table, a combination of a rectangular and circular-shaped desk that encourages CSRs to

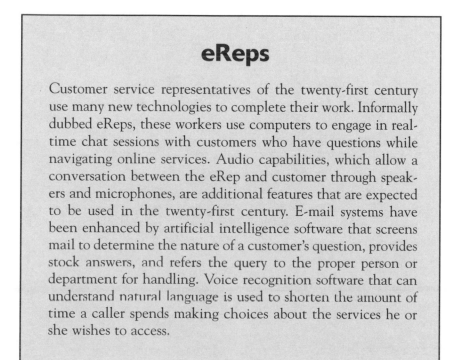

eReps

Customer service representatives of the twenty-first century use many new technologies to complete their work. Informally dubbed eReps, these workers use computers to engage in real-time chat sessions with customers who have questions while navigating online services. Audio capabilities, which allow a conversation between the eRep and customer through speakers and microphones, are additional features that are expected to be used in the twenty-first century. E-mail systems have been enhanced by artificial intelligence software that screens mail to determine the nature of a customer's question, provides stock answers, and refers the query to the proper person or department for handling. Voice recognition software that can understand natural language is used to shorten the amount of time a caller spends making choices about the services he or she wishes to access.

scoot beside their customers when they are doing business such as filling out new account forms or reviewing a bank statement. Chairs are on wheels to allow for flexible grouping to serve a married couple or business partners. From a small counter at the front of the branch, CSRs take care of simple transactions. As described by journalist Steve Cocheo, check cashing takes place there because the counter is designed so that "the rear of the . . . counter's backdrop contains . . . teller cash dispensers." To complete more complicated work, the CSRs "excuse themselves and go to their desk in the branch's nonpublic backshop, or 'bullpen,' where each employee runs their own till."[72]

Call Centers

Technology is creating other radical changes in work settings that will continue to reduce the need for traditional tellers. Banks

In recent years, banks have come to rely on CSRs like those at this call center to provide customers with service over the telephone.

increasingly provide service through call centers, centralized units (or, in some cases, separate companies that specialize in providing these services to other companies) that handle service calls and which are staffed by CSRs. In these centers CSRs wear telephone headsets and continually take calls from customers who need information, wish to lodge a complaint, open an account, or add services to existing accounts. They may refer to scripts—paper versions or those that pop up on their computer screens—when dealing with certain typical situations.

Writer Joe Fleischer observes that more financial services companies are seeing the role of the CSR as one that cuts across the entire institution. "Financial institutions are starting to unify branch staff, call center agents and on-line representatives into customer service groups."[73] Thus CSRs will find that their job responsibilities are increasingly defined by the overall needs of the institutions where they work and by their work relationship with technology. Thus old measures of a CSR's job performance, such as how long each call takes, will give way to factors such as how the CSR fits in with an overall plan that includes not simply answering questions but selling services and making the most valuable customers happy.

Technology Partners

CSRs working at call centers use computers with many different capabilities, depending on the company. Their workstations are actually "partners" in the sense that they allow CSRs to obtain and track the information they need. For example, they may place calls and schedule a second call that will allow the CSR to follow up on whatever went on in the first call: If a CSR suggests that a customer consolidate debt with a home equity loan and the customer said it would first be necessary to consult with his or her spouse, the CSR can receive a prompt to call the customer back at the appropriate time. Customer relations management expert Diane Gerstner points out that some of the more sophisticated systems include "automated number identification, pop-up screens that display the caller's account information, [and] on-line deposit and loan rate sheets."[74]

Other technologies with which CSRs partner are the recorded messages and phone trees that customers navigate on their way to talking with a CSR. Representatives may be asked to participate in planning the tone and content of these messages. Jack Armstrong, a consultant who specializes in improving the effectiveness of recorded messages, highly recommends input from CSRs because they are the ones who first interact with customers who dial through the automated systems. Thus CSRs can share their experiences about "exactly what [customers] want when they call [and] what kind of mood they're in when they reach a CSR."[75]

Keeping Informed

Information is the most important job tool for CSRs working in call centers. They use a number of different ways to access the information they need to answer questions, including the institution's account and loan databases for questions that relate to a particular customer. CSRs also handle general questions, many of which are asked over and over again. Some companies devise methods that allow quick access to answers to commonly asked questions. One company uses basic computer programs to assemble a giant "Answer Guide" that CSRs can access using keyword searches. Some companies have developed "canned" answers to typical questions that can be inserted into e-mail messages.

One frequent reason for a call from a customer is that he or she may not remember the amount or purpose of a check that was written but not entered in the customer's checkbook register. Researching this information can be time consuming for CSRs. However, banks are now beginning to make images of checks that are stored online for access by either a customer or a CSR. This results in a dramatic time savings. Bank executive Earl Jennings describes how CSRs use the imaging system at his bank: "It's so time consuming to deal with a bank that isn't image-enabled when it comes to a question about a check that's floating somewhere in the system. Our members are able to pull up the image in the first phone call and say, 'Hey, you wrote check number 171 to the tutor.'"[76]

Thinking on Their Feet

Whether they are researching answers to account questions or handling an upset customer, CSRs must have excellent interpersonal skills and the ability to think on their feet (and while talking on the phone or responding to an online inquiry). Call

Improving Skills and Status

Customer service representatives (CSRs) are often invisible employees whose job challenges and professionalism are underappreciated. In an effort to help CSRs develop their skills the International Customer Service Association (ICSA), which supports the industry through networking and education, has developed a certification program, which it describes this way:

The primary goal of the ICSA Professional Certification Program is to increase the level of customer service. Your customer service team will receive empowerment that only comes from increased confidence and knowledge of job skills. They will have a greater understanding of new technology, and a deeper appreciation of customer concerns. Additionally, you will be able to promote the fact that your customer service team members are certified professionals, CCSPs [certified customer service professionals] to be exact. And suddenly, where there was no encompassing title, you have a highly educated, designated professional staff.

center representatives must be able to judge when the conversation is becoming inefficient and steer the customer to finish up. However, sometimes a personal touch can help improve business relationships. One journalist paraphrased a consultant's thoughts on this issue in these words: "There is a fine line between gabbing too much . . . and trying to get the member off the phone quickly."[77] Because CSRs are often judged by how many calls they can handle in a given period of time, walking this line successfully is critical to their success.

Being able to solve problems while a customer waits requires not only a calm demeanor but also skill at using company databases to access information and a familiarity with company policies. Companies value the employees with the most skill because they can deftly handle the most difficult situations. In fact financial institutions are using technology to make sure that their best workers are linked to the best customers. Automated phone systems are

Banks typically employ the latest in computer technology. Customer service representatives must master this technology to be successful.

being developed that allow an incoming call to be routed to a CSR based on the customer's track record with the institution and the reason for the call. The best CSRs will be given the opportunity to serve those customers who are the most potentially profitable for the company; for example, someone with good savings who is seeking a large loan rather than a customer who wants to check an account balance.

Computer and Sales Skills a Must

Because so much of their work involves using, or helping others to use, technology, CSRs and tellers in the twenty-first century must have the ability to master technology and to learn new ways of using existing technology. "Traditionally, customer service agents have been hired for their oral communication skills. But the Web may require lenders to have people with Internet and writing skills as well,"[78] reports journalist Ted Cornwell after interviewing company executives about their expectations.

Tellers and CSRs must also have excellent sales skills because they are increasingly asked to market financial services products to customers. In fact some calls centers are specifically geared to handling not only customer service, but also sales calls made by, or to, customers. The ability to sell is therefore critical. Gerstner believes that CSR qualifications include "a good phone voice . . . and grace under pressure." Nevertheless for her, "intelligence and a winning sales personality are the most important attributes for an effective call center representative."[79]

Education

Tellers and CSRs need high school diplomas, which they may earn through school or by completing the requirements necessary for a general education diploma (GED). They do not typically need college degrees. However, some employers look for CSRs or tellers who have taken classes in finance or marketing at universities or community colleges. CSRs and tellers who have completed coursework in computer technology will be particularly desirable. CSRs and tellers learn on the job, either through formal training programs or by mentoring within the institution's branch or call center. In addition they may take courses through professional associations, either online or in seminar or lecture settings. The American Bankers Association (ABA) is one group that conducts excellent training programs for beginning CSRs and tellers or for those with experience who are interested in honing their skills. One example is a course in telephone etiquette, which according to an online course description covers topics including how to use "appropriate language during telephone conversations" and how to use "an effective approach to handle unintentional disconnects."[80]

Advancement and Salary

Experienced CSRs and tellers can rise to supervisory positions within the bank branch. In call centers and in electronic support settings, CSRs who supervise others have duties such as checking the quality of the contacts made by listening in to calls or looking at incoming and outgoing e-mails. Supervisors set goals for the numbers of calls employees should make or the level of professional service they should give in a branch and encourage employees to meet these goals. They may organize meetings or find ways to motivate CSRs through contests or games that reward excellent service. With college training CSRs can rise to more general management positions within the institution.

The Bureau of Labor Statistics reports that in 2001 CSRs in all businesses earned a median annual salary of $25,400. Low salaries were in the $16,700 range, with high salaries in the $42,100 range. In *Banking, Finance, and Insurance*, author Thomas Fitch estimates that the average salary range for banking CSRs is $19,000 to $20,000 annually. Tellers, who often work part-time, earned a median wage of $9.21 an hour in 2000, according to the Bureau of Labor Statistics.

Matters out of Their Control

Low pay is one of the chief drawbacks of these jobs. In addition, because many CSRs and tellers work part-time hours they may not have benefits, such as health insurance, that are offered to full-time employees. CSRs, especially at call centers open twenty-four hours, may work unusual hours. Those who work in grocery stores and other atypical locations can expect to be scheduled for evening and weekend work.

While compensation and hours may not be highly desirable, the most difficult aspect of the CSR's job is dealing with customers who are upset over something the institution has done or at the length of time they have to wait to meet with a CSR in a

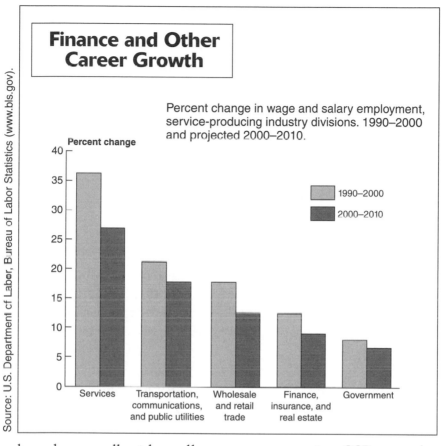

Finance and Other Career Growth

Percent change in wage and salary employment, service-producing industry divisions. 1990–2000 and projected 2000–2010.

Legend: 1990–2000, 2000–2010

Source: U.S. Department of Labor, Bureau of Labor Statistics (www.bls.gov).

branch or to talk with a call center representative. CSRs may also be challenged because different customers have different expectations. For example, while young customers who cut their teeth on computers are satisfied with speed in their interactions with CSRs, older customers still expect the personal approach they became familiar with when they first started banking. These customers prefer to be "greeted with a smile and by name,"[81] (as described in a *Credit Union Journal* article) which can be difficult at the end of a long, high-stress day.

These and certain other problems—such as not having the information they need to answer customer questions—are out of the CSRs' control, and this can cause frustration, especially since these workers are expected to remain polite no matter what the customer says. Also workstations can be confining or uncomfortable, although some companies are installing ergonomic chairs. And call center representatives are especially prone to stress because they are typically trapped in a cubicle and tethered to the phone all day (or all night if they work for an institution with twenty-four-hour live support for customers). Some employers, however, are trying to improve such working conditions by offering comforts like recliners and television lounges for breaks. "It's a high-stress job, and it's really important for them to be able to go to a completely different environment,"[82] says consultant Paul Barrath.

Finding Solutions

While creative work environments are pleasing to CSRs, the work itself has many positive aspects. For example, acting as a CSR is a good way for someone without a college degree to become familiar with the banking environment. This can help CSRs decide if they wish to pursue a career in that setting or obtain additional education to allow for advancement. Not all interactions with customers are unpleasant either. CSRs feel satisfied when they are able to meet the needs of a customer and the bank by initiating what they hope will be a long-term relationship. In addition, successful research on a customer's question can give a CSR a sense of accomplishment.

Some institutions allow CSRs to exercise independence in their work, allowing for a sense of personal accomplishment. For example, one credit union allows CSRs to act independently in resolving certain kinds of customer complaints. A situation in which this may occur is, for instance, when a customer complains about a monthly service charge that was imposed on a checking account. If, after researching the account history on the credit union's database, the CSR discovers that the fee would not have applied except for the fact that the credit union delayed crediting a deposit made by the customer, the CSR can decide on the spot to waive the fee and give the money back to the customer (usually by making a credit to the account). Another credit union may have a policy that requires the CSR to get the approval of a manager before making this decision.

The role of CSRs will continue to expand in the twenty-first century when customers are expected to be harder to please and easier to lose because they have choices not only of bank branches but of a seemingly unlimited array of online services. Journalist

David Rountree sums up the importance of managing customer relationships this way: "There is a consensus among bankers today that if customers haven't always been king, they certainly will be in the 21st century, especially in the financial services industry."[83]

17. Fox, *Starting and Building Your Own Accounting Business*, p. 18.

18. Cynthia Harrington, "In an Age of Specialization, More CPAs Are Staking Claims in 'Narrower-Focus' Practices," *Accounting Today*, August 6, 2001, p. 39.

19. Fox, *Starting and Building Your Own Accounting Business*, p. 297.

20. Cohen, *Accountant's Guide to the Internet*, p. 202.

21. Andrew Denka, "Ask Andy Advice Column," American Institute of Certified Public Accoutants, April 29, 2003. www.aicpa.org.

22. James A. Cashin, *Careers and Opportunities in Accounting*. New York: E.P. Dutton, 1965, pp. 76–77.

Chapter Two: Financial Planners

23. Certified Financial Planner Board of Standards, Inc., "Financial Planning Basics," 2003. www.cfp.net.

24. Shelley A. Lee, "What Is Financial Planning, Anyway?" *Journal of Financial Planning*, December 2001. www.fpanet.org.

25. Quoted in Richard F. Stolz, "The Many Facets of Client Reviews," *Journal of Financial Planning*, May 2003. www.fpanet.org.

26. Certified Financial Planner Board of Standards, Inc. "Financial Planning Process," 2003. www.cfp.net.

27. Charles E. Foster II, telephone interview by author, Del Mar, CA, June 2003.

28. Foster, telephone interview.

29. Quoted in Stolz, "The Many Facets of Client Reviews."

30. Quoted in Stolz, "The Many Facets of Client Reviews."

31. Foster, telephone interview.

32. Michael B. Horwitz, "Reality Check: A Natural Approach to Dealing with Clients Emphasizes the Need to Be Real, Rather Than Scripted," *Financial Planning*, May 1, 2003.

33. Quoted in Jacqueline M. Quinn, "Marketing Tactics Examined," *Journal of Financial Planning*, September 2001. www.fpanet.org.

34. Quoted in Quinn, "Marketing Tactics Examined."

35. Quinn, "Marketing Tactics Examined."

36. Harrington, "In An Age of Specialization, More CPAs Are Staking Claims in 'Narrower-Focus' Practices," p. 39.

37. Quoted in Catherine Newton, "Making Connections: How Planners Manage Their Technology Needs," *Journal of Financial Planning*, August 2000. www.fpanet.org.

38. Quoted in Newton, "Workshop: New Kids on the Block: Freshman Planners Share Their Experiences," *Journal of Financial Planning*, September 2001. www.fpanet.org.

39. Foster, telephone interview.

40. Quoted in Newton, "Workshop."

41. Quoted in Shelly A. Lee, "Dear Mr. Chairman," *Journal of Financial Planning*, November 2001. www.fpanet.org.

42. Quoted in Newton, "Workshop."

43. Quoted in Newton, "Workshop."

Chapter Three: Debt Collectors

44. Federal Trade Commission, "Fair Debt Collection," March 1999. www.ftc.gov.

45. Brian Leaf, "Bad Times Good for Debt Agencies," *Crain's Chicago Business*, October 14, 2002, p. SB-11.

46. Quoted in Denise A. Carabet, "5 Commercial Agencies to Watch: Business Collections Pays Off," *Collection and Credit Risk*, July 1999, pp. 20+.

47. Quoted in *Credit Collection News*, "Collecting from the Dead Can Be Profitable," January 1999, pp. 1+.

48. J.W. Dysart, "Shopping for Commercial Collections Agencies," *Collections & Credit Risk*, May 1999, pp. 74+.

49. Quoted in Kris Hunter, "Beyond the Power Dialer," *Credit Card Management*, November 1996, pp. 120+.

50. Trevor Curwin, "The Credit Store Pans for Chargeoff Gold," *Private Placement Report*, April 12, 1999, p. 6.

51. Quoted in Lisa Fickenscher, "No More Mr. Bad Guy: In a Switch Collection Agents Soften Approach," *American Banker*, October 22, 1999, pp. 1+.

52. Burney Simpson, "A Not-So-Simple Labor Market," *Credit Card Management*, October 2001, pp. 52+.

53. Fair Debt Collection Practices Act. "Consumer Information," August 13, 2003. www.ftc.gov.

54. Quoted in Leaf, "Bad Times Good for Debt Agencies," p. SB-11.

55. Quoted in Kate Fitzgerald, "No More Frugal Paymaster," *Collections & Credit Risk*, October 1998, pp. 23+.

56. F. Romall Smalls, "Recovering Losses," *Black Enterprise*, June 1999, pp. 52+.

57. Quoted in Fitzgerald, "No More Frugal Paymaster."

Chapter Four: Stockbrokers

58. Andrew A. Lanyi, *Confessions of a Stockbroker*. Paramus, NJ: Prentice Hall, 1984, p. 217.

59. Federal Reserve Board, *Summary of Commentary on Current Economic Conditions*, July 30, 2003. www.federalreserve.gov.

60. Quoted in eFinancial Careers, "Day in the Life: Carine de Boissezon, Equities Saleswoman," June 2003. www.efinancial careers.com.

61. Quoted in *On Wall Street*, "Bogle on Brokers," November 1, 2000, p. 168.

62. Quoted in Tony Chapelle, "Lions of Wall Street—Getting Rich Slow," *On Wall Street*, September 2000.

63. New York Stock Exchange, Inc., "The New York Stock Exchange: A Guide to the World's Leading Securities Market," 2002. www.nyse.com.

64. Quoted in Evan Cooper, "Roaring Harry Dent," *On Wall Street*, June 2000, pp. 46+.

65. Quoted in Daniel Marcus, "Combating the Online Invasion," *On Wall Street, Guide to Independent Broker-Dealers Supplement*, September 1999, pp. 28+.

66. Quoted in Marcus, "Combating the Online Invasion."

67. U.S. Securities and Exchange Commission, "The Investor's Advocate: How the SEC Protects Investors and Maintains

Market Integrity," March 19, 2003. www.sec.gov.

68. National Association of Securities Dealers, Inc. "Prohibited Conduct," October 18, 2000. www.nasd.com.

Chapter Five: Tellers and Customer Service Representatives

69. *American Banker*, "Branch Personnel Lead Customers to the Web," November 22, 2002, pp. 1+.

70. Quoted in John J. Lafkas and Larry W. Hunter, "Opening the Box: Information Technology, Work Practices, and Wages," "*Industrial and Labor Relations Review*, January 2003, pp. 224+.

71. Lafkas and Hunter, "Opening the Box."

72. Steve Cocheo, "Why Is This Banker Quacking? Why Can't You Find a Teller in His New Branch? And Why Do All the Chairs Have Wheels?" *ABA Banking Journal*, June 2002, pp. 16(4)+.

73. Joe Fleischer, "Case Studies—Financial Services—The Top Currency in Financial Services," *Call Center*, February 1, 2003, p. 42.

74. Diane Gerstner, "Higher Calling: Here Are Five Steps That a Bank Can Take to Develop a Call Center Strategy to Improve Customer Outreach and Enhance Sales," *ABA Banking Journal*, April 2002, pp. 22(4)+.

75. Jack Armstrong, "The Invisible Employee Consumers Love to Hate," *Customer Relationship Management*, October 2002, p. 19.

76. Quoted in *ABA Banking Journal*, "Check Images Take a Bigger Role: Customer Convenience and Customer Service Are Both Big Gainers," March 2003, pp. 51+.

77. *Credit Union Journal*, "Call Center Not a 'Cost Center,' Says One Expert," November 25, 2002, pp. 14+.

78. Ted Cornwell, "Don't Just Call, Interact," *Bank Technology News*, October 2000, pp. 34+.

79. Gerstner, "Higher Calling."

80. American Bankers Association, "ABA Performance Training Series: Telephone Etiquette." www.aba.com.

81. Neil Goldman, "Smiles May Go Miles, but It's Research That Delivers," *Credit Union Journal*, February 3, 2003, pp. 4+.

82. Quoted in *Credit Union Journal*, "Retention-Getter: How Some Credit Unions Are Making Changes to the Physical Workplace to Ensure Employees Remain Happy," January 13, 2003, pp. 1+.

83. David Rountree, "CRM the Hard Way," *Bank Technology News*, May 3, 2002, pp. 1+.

Organizations to Contact

American Institute of Certified Public Accountants (AICPA)
1211 Avenue of the Americas
New York, NY 10036-8775
(212) 596-6200
www.aicpa.org

Professional organization of certified public accountants. Provides educational programs and ethics counseling. Advocates for the profession's interests and sets performance standards.

Association of Credit and Collection Professionals (ACA International)
P.O. Box 390106
Minneapolis, MN 55439
(952) 926-6547
www.collector.com

An advocacy, networking, and education association for collection professionals. Its website includes news items related to the field.

Financial Planning Association (FPA)
5775 Glenridge Drive, NE
Suite B-300
Atlanta, GA 30328
(800) 322-4237
www.fpanet.org

An advocacy and education association that publishes the *Journal of Financial Planning*.

International Customer Service Association (ICSA)
401 North Michigan Avenue
Chicago, IL 60611
(800) 360-4272
www.icsa.com

Promotes awareness of the customer-care industry and the development of its members through networking, education, and research.

Finance

New York Stock Exchange (NYSE)
11 Wall Street
New York, NY 10005
(212) 656-3000
www.nyse.com

The world's best known securities exchange offers outstanding educational tours, teacher seminars, as well as educational materials and posters by mail and online.

Securities Industry Association (SIA)
1425 K Street, NW, 7th floor
Washington, DC 20005-3500
(202) 216-2000
www.sia.com

Investment banking, brokerage, and mutual fund firms are members of this organization, which provides advocacy and education opportunities and conducts surveys and provides consultations on issues of interest to its members.

For Further Reading

Books

Thomas Fitch, *Career Opportunities in Banking, Finance, and Insurance*. New York: Checkmark Books, 2002. Well organized, concise descriptions of dozens of jobs in banking, finance, and insurance, including employment prospects and salaries.

Trudy Ring, *Careers in Finance*. Lincolnwood, IL: VGM Career Horizons, 1993. Discussions of finance careers, including comments by those working in the field. Has practical information such as sample résumés and cover letters, and a list of colleges and universities that offer finance and banking programs.

U.S. Department of Labor, *Occupational Outlook Handbook, 2002–2003*. Washington, DC: Bureau of Labor Statistics, 2002. A primary sourcebook for career information. Includes up-to-date summaries of more than two hundred careers, with information on job duties, outlook, required training and education, and salaries.

WetFeet Insider Guide to Careers in Accounting, 2004 Edition. San Francisco: Wet Feet, 2003. A hip, up-to-date manual that brings accounting work to life. This book can also be downloaded at www.wetfeet.com.

Websites

AICPA: Accounting: A Career Without Boundaries. (www. aicpa.org/nolimits/index.htm). Site of the Student Affiliate Program of the American Institute of Certified Public Accountants. Readable career information including profiles of accounting professionals and an advice column.

America's Career InfoNet (www.acinet.org). Government-sponsored website that contains lots of easy-to-access information about careers, education, wages, and employers. Includes links to fifty-five hundred online career sources and has 360 career-specific videos that can be downloaded.

New York Stock Exchange (www.nyse.com). The exchange's website has excellent educational information about the process of investing and trading.

students.gov (www.students.gov). Federal government gateway includes information about a wide range of careers, with links to dozens of related websites.

Works Consulted

Books

Jason Alba and Manisha Bathija, *Vault Career Guide to Accounting*. Vault Career Library, 2002. One of the most current, industry-focused career guides.

John Bartlett, *Familiar Quotations, Fourteenth Edition*. Boston: Little, Brown, 1968. A famous reference book of quotations.

John W. Buckley and Marlene H. Buckley, *The Accounting Profession*. Los Angeles: Melville Publishing, 1974. A statistically supported evaluation of accounting careers, including history, attitudes, work tools, and ethical responsibilities.

James A. Cashin, *Careers and Opportunities in Accounting*. New York: E.P. Dutton, 1965. While the career data is dated, this book contains helpful information about the personal characteristics needed for success in accounting.

Eric E. Cohen, *Accountant's Guide to the Internet*. New York: John Wiley & Sons, 1997. An excellent detailed road map to using the Internet in an accounting practice.

Jack Fox, *Starting and Building Your Own Accounting Business*. New York: John Wiley & Sons, 1991. Thorough guide to the steps needed to succeed in one's own accounting business.

Andrew A. Lanyi, *Confessions of a Stockbroker*. Paramus, NJ: Prentice Hall, 1984. An engaging discussion of this famous stockbroker's career, and tips for wise investing.

Joel G. Siegel and Jae K. Shim, *Accounting Handbook*. Hauppauge, NY: Barron's Educational Series, 2000. A weighty, authoritative reference book for accountants that covers concepts and definitions relating to all aspects of accounting work.

Dian G. Smith, *Women in Finance*. Skokie, IL: VGM Career Horizons, 1981. Profiles of successful women in the field, including an investment manager, public accountant, stockbroker, and financial editor.

John A. Tracy, *Accounting for Dummies*, Foster City, CA: IDG Books Worldwide, 1997. A thorough but readable insider's view of the work of accountants. Important points are highlighted in lists and summaries.

Shari H. Wescott and Robert E. Seiler, *Women in the Accounting Profession*. New York: Markus Wiener, 1986. Insightful overview of the status of women in accounting, historically and into the 1980s. Includes helpful information about the expectations and challenges all accountants face, and the personal characteristics needed to succeed.

Periodicals

ABA *Banking Journal*, "Check Images Take a Bigger Role: Customer Convenience and Customer Service Are Both Big Gainers," March 2003.

American Banker, "Branch Personnel Lead Customers to the Web," November 22, 2002.

Jack Armstrong, "The Invisible Employee Consumers Love to Hate," *Customer Relationship Management*, October 2002.

Denise A. Carabet, "5 Commercial Agencies to Watch: Business Collections Pays Off," *Collection and Credit Risk*, July 1999.

Tony Chapelle, "Lions of Wall Street—Getting Rich Slow," *On Wall Street*, September 2000.

Steve Cocheo, "Why Is This Banker Quacking? Why Can't You Find a Teller in His New Branch? And Why Do All the Chairs Have Wheels?" ABA *Banking Journal*, June 2002.

Evan Cooper, "Roaring Harry Dent," *On Wall Street*, June 2000.

Ted Cornwell, "Don't Just Call, Interact,"*Bank Technology News*, October 2000.

Credit Collection News, "Collecting From the Dead Can Be Profitable," January 1999.

Credit Union Journal, "Call Center Not a 'Cost Center,' Says One Expert," November 25, 2002.

————, "Retention-Getter: How Some Credit Unions Are Making Changes to the Physical Workplace to Ensure Employees Remain Happy," January 13, 2003.

Trevor Curwin, "The Credit Store Pans for Chargeoff Gold," *Private Placement Report*, April 12, 1999.

J.W. Dysart, "Shopping for Commercial Collections Agencies," *Collections & Credit Risk*, May 1999.

Lisa Fickenscher, "No More Mr. Bad Guy: In a Switch Collection Agents Soften Approach," *American Banker*, October 22, 1999.

Kate Fitzgerald, "No More Frugal Paymaster," *Collections & Credit Risk*, October 1998.

Joe Fleischer, "Case Studies—Financial Services—The Top Currency in Financial Services," *Call Center*, February 1, 2003.

Diane Gerstner, "Higher Calling: Here Are Five Steps That a Bank Can Take to Develop a Call Center Strategy to Improve Customer Outreach and Enhance Sales," *ABA Banking Journal*, April 2002.

Neil Goldman, "Smiles May Go Miles, but It's Research That Delivers," *Credit Union Journal*, February 3, 2003.

Cynthia Harrington, "In an Age of Specialization, More CPAs Are Staking Claims in 'Narrower-Focus' Practices," *Accounting Today*, August 6, 2001.

Michael B. Horwitz, "Reality Check: A Natural Approach to Dealing with Clients Emphasizes the Need to Be Real, Rather than Scripted," *Financial Planning*, May 1, 2003.

Kris Hunter, "Beyond the Power Dialer," *Credit Card Management*, November 1996.

John J. Lafkas and Larry W. Hunter, "Opening the Box: Information Technology, Work Practices, and Wages," *Industrial and Labor Relations Review*, January 2003.

Brian Leaf, "Bad Times Good for Debt Agencies," *Crain's Chicago Business*, October 14, 2002.

Daniel Marcus, "Combating the Online Invasion," *On Wall Street, Guide to Independent Broker-Dealers Supplement*, September 1999.

Suzanne McGee, "Wrong Numbers," *Red Herring*, March 2003.

On Wall Street, "Bogle on Brokers," November 1, 2000.

David Rountree, "CRM the Hard Way," *Bank Technology News*, May 3, 2002.

Burney Simpson, "A Not-So-Simple Labor Market," *Credit Card Management*, October 2001.

F. Romall Smalls, "Recovering Losses," *Black Enterprise*, June 1999.

Internet Sources

American Bankers Association, "ABA Performance Training Series: Telephone Etiquette." www.aba.com.

American Institute of Certified Public Accountants, "Career Paths." www.aicpa.org.

Bureau of Labor Statistics, "Tellers," *Occupational Outlook Handbook*. www.bls.gov.

Certified Financial Planner Board of Standards, Inc., "Common Questions About Financial Planning." www.cfp.net.

———, "Financial Planning Basics," 2003. www.cfp.net.

———, "Financial Planning Process," 2003. www.cfp.net.

Deloitte Touche Tohmatsu, "Job Title: Senior International Tax Senior," 2003. http://careers.deloitte.com.

Andrew Denka, "Ask Andy Advice Column," American Institute of Certified Public Accountants, April 29, 2003. www.aicpa.org.

eFinancial Careers, "Day in the Life: Carine de Boissezon, Equities Saleswoman," June 2003. www.efinancialcareers.com.

Fair Debt Collection Practices Act. "Consumer Information," August 13, 2003. www.ftc.gov.

Federal Reserve Board, *Summary of Commentary on Current Economic Conditions*, July 30, 2003. www.federal reserve.gov.

Federal Trade Commission, "Fair Debt Collection," March 1999. www.ftc.gov.

Shelley A. Lee, "Dear Mr. Chairman," *Journal of Financial Planning*, November 2001. www.fpanet.org.

———, "What Is Financial Planning, Anyway?" *Journal of Financial Planning*, December 2001. www.fpanet.org.

National Association of Securities Dealers, "Prohibited Conduct," October 18, 2000. www.nasd.com.

Catherine Newton, "Making Connections: How Planners Manage Their Technology Needs," *Journal of Financial Planning*, August 2000. www.fpanet.org.

————, "Workshop: New Kids on the Block: Freshman Planners Share Their Experiences," *Journal of Financial Planning*, September 2001. www.fpanet.org.

New York Stock Exchange, Inc., "The New York Stock Exchange: A Guide to the World's Leading Securities Market," 2002. www.nyse.com.

Jacqueline M. Quinn, "Marketing Tactics Examined," *Journal of Financial Planning*, September 2001. www.fpanet.org.

Richard F. Stolz, "The Many Facets of Client Reviews," *Journal of Financial Planning*, May 2003. www.fpanet.org.

U.S. Securities and Exchange Commission, "The Investor's Advocate: How the SEC Protects Investors and Maintains Market Integrity," March 19, 2003. www.sec.gov.

WetFeet.com, "Accounting, Career Overview," 2003. www.wetfeet.com.

Interviews

Catherine Allen, e-mail interview by author, June 2003.

Charles E. Foster II, telephone interview by author, Del Mar, CA, June 2003.

Claude Organ, telephone interview by author, Del Mar, CA, June 2003.

Index

accountants, public versus private, 13

accounts
checking, 73
tracking, 49–50

advertising. *See* marketing

advice
age and sources of, 36
public accountants and, 17, 18
stockbrokers and, 57, 62–64, 67
see also consulting function

American Bankers Association, 83–84

American Institute of Certified Public Accountants (AICPA)
on assurance services, 22
Code of Professional Conduct, 17
as resource, 16

artificial intelligence software, 77

assets, 32

assurance services, 22

audits, 19–21

banks, nontraditional
branch offices of, 74

bear market, 70

Bloomberg machines, 59

bonds, 57

bull market, 70

call centers, 78–80, 86

certification and licensing
of customer service representatives, 81
of financial planners, 41–42
see also CPAs; education, experience, and pay

Certified Financial Planner Board of Standards Inc., 30, 33, 41, 44

characteristics, desired. *See* qualities, desired

checking accounts, opening, 73

clients
financial planners and, 30–32, 40
public accountants and, 17–18
stockbrokers and, 62–66

cold calls, 66, 71

companies
contacting, about debts, 48
financial audits of, 19–21
multinational, consulting with, 22–23
see also stocks, shares of

consulting function
accountants and, 13, 21–23, 24
multinational companies and, 22–23
see also advice

controllers, 27

CPAs (certified public

judgment, professional
financial planners and,
41–42
public accountants and, 17
stockbrokers and, 68–70

large firms, working for,
24–25, 26
legally enforceable, 14
limit orders, 64

marketing
financial planners and,
36–38
public accountants and, 26
see also selling services
market orders, 64
meetings, with financial
planners, 32, 34, 35
multinational companies,
consulting with, 22–23
mutual funds, 57, 59

National Association of
Securities Dealers, 43,
69–70
needs, client-specific
financial planners and,
30–32, 40
public accountants and,
17–18
stockbrokers and, 62–66
networking, public accountants and, 26
New York Stock Exchange
(NYSE)
specialists and, 65
stockbrokers and, 57

Trading Floor, 58

online stock trading, 67
over-the-counter stocks, 57,
65

partner, 24–25
partnerships and public
accountants, 25–26
place of work. *See* workplace
plans, 33–35
portfolios, balanced, 62
predictive dialers, 49–50, 55
probate proceedings, 48–49

qualities, desired
in customer service representatives, 80–81, 83
in debt collectors, 47,
51–52
in financial planners,
35–36
in public accountants, 29
in stockbrokers, 63, 66–67,
71

recorded messages, 79–80
regulation, government
financial planners and, 43
stockbrokers and, 59, 69
see also Fair Debt
Collection Practices Act
research function
public accountants and,
15–18
stockbrokers and, 59–61
retail brokering, 59

Picture Credits

Cover image: © AFP/CORBIS
Daniel Acker/Bloomberg News/Landov, 60
AP/Wide World Photos, 16
© Bill Aron/Photo Edit, Inc., 11
© William A. Bake/CORBIS, 20
Corel, 58
© Darama/CORBIS, 41
© Mary Kate Denny/Photo Edit, Inc., 75
© Jon Feingersh/CORBIS, 53
© Reuters/Landov, 78
© Bonnie Kamin/Photo Edit, Inc., 74
David Karp/Bloomberg News/Landov, 65
© Tom & Dee Ann McCarthy/CORBIS, 49
Photodisc, 31, 64
Picture History, 14
© H. Prinz/CORBIS, 37
© Mark Richards/Photo Edit, Inc., 82
© Bob Rowan; Progressive Image/CORBIS, 24
© Chuck Savage/CORBIS, 28
© David Young-Wolff/Photo Edit, Inc., 34, 68
Steve Zmina, 12, 46, 85

About the Author

Patrice Cassedy is the author of Lucent Books's *Understanding Flowers for Algernon* and *Teen Pregnancy*, as well as several of the publisher's career books, including *Biotechnology* and *Education*. Before publishing her first book, Cassedy wrote many articles on subjects including the craft of writing and family safety. She worked nearly twenty years as a lawyer for financial institutions, taught law school, and completed courses in marketing and retailing. She enjoys guiding young people as they discover their career passions, especially her high school–age daughter, Eva, who is interested in adolescent psychology, and her son, Michael, who is a jazz pianist.